THE
GARLIC LOVERS'
COOKBOOK
Volume II

from
GILROY

Garlic Capital of the World

Celestial Arts
Berkeley, California

Celestial Arts
P.O. Box 7327
Berkeley, California 94707

First Printing, July 1985

Cover design: Ken Scott
Cover photograph: Robert R. Stein
Interior design: Abigail Johnston, Nancy Austin
Interior illustrations: Nancy Austin
Composition: HMS Typography, Inc.

Made in the United States of America

Gilroy Garlic Festival Committee.
        The garlic lovers cookbook, Volume II

ISBN 0-89087-424-7 (comb bind)

5 — 96 95 94

ACKNOWLEDGMENT

In keeping with the spirit of the Gilroy Garlic Festival, The Garlic Lovers' Cookbook, Volume II has been made possible through sharing and volunteerism.

It began with the creative entrants in the Great Garlic Recipe Contest and Cook-off sharing their treasured recipes. Then the volunteers devoted hours, even days, to the task of reading, examining and classifying each recipe. The selection process was also one of sharing as the volunteer cooks chose and prepared the dishes for their families and friends to taste and critique.

The Gilroy Garlic Festival wishes to express special gratitude to these generous individuals whose contributions have made it possible to publish The Garlic Lovers' Cookbook, Volume II. Special thanks, also, to Karen Christopher, Garlic Festival Cookbook Coordinator and Caryl Saunders Associates for their professional input.

Without the altruistic attitude of so many people this book and its predecessor, The Garlic Lovers' Cookbook, would not be nearly so interesting nor inclusive of so many great ideas for cooking with garlic . . . and with love.

Gilroy Garlic Festival Association Inc.
P. O. Box 2311
Gilroy, California 95020
(408) 842-1625

DEDICATION

To the people of Gilroy
For sharing a lifestyle of
        good food, good times
        and for giving from the heart.

Contents

The People of Gilroy

Garlic now gives the town (Gilroy) a certain dignity . . . .

The Wall Street Journal

The first reviews were great! "The ultimate in summer food fairs" *(Los Angeles Herald Examiner)*; "Fame is Nothing to Sniff at in Gilroy" *(Washington Post)*; ". . . Call the town of Gilroy fragrant and friendly" (Copely News Service); "It was rollicking good fun and the food was super" *(San Francisco Chronicle)*; "By any measure, it was a success" *(San Francisco Examiner)*. The nationwide headlines, proclaiming the phenomenal success of the first Garlic Festival in 1979 caught the people of Gilroy, California by surprise.

When a group of local residents staged the first weekend celebration of the "scented pearl" to increase community pride and help create a more flavorable image of their town, little did they know what a dramatic impact it would make on Gilroy. What they did know was how to use the area's most prominent product, garlic. They knew how to cook up cauldrons of mouthwatering garlic-laced food, how to have fun with garlic, how to motivate people and how to share this very special lifestyle. The rest is history and the Garlic Festival became a permanent fixture on the town calender.

The response to Gilroy's harvest festival surpassed even the most optimistic expectations. Yearly attendance grew from 20,000 to 120,000 and by 1985 over one-half million visitors had trekked to Gilroy, "The Garlic Capital of the World," to share in the culinary legacy of its townspeople.

The steering committee of community leaders, determined to provide a quality event, rose to meet the challenges created by the ever-increasing numbers of garlic lovers. More garlic! More space! More food! More planning! More volunteers! All this, and a more enviable challenge: determine the best use for the monies generated at each year's event.

More garlic? No problem in Gilroy. The issue of more space? Solved with cooperation from the City of Gilroy's award-winning Parks Department and the generosity of local landowners. To meet the other needs a cross section of Gilroy residents came forward as volunteers to form thirty committees to deal with the creative aspects, detailed planning, logistics and implementation of each phase of the festival. The Gilroy Garlic Festival Association was formed as a nonprofit, tax exempt private corporation with a rotating board of directors. The Association's continuing goal was identified as the support of community projects, charitable groups and service organizations. Several criteria were established for the disbursement of Festival funds, but the majority of funds available is given to those groups who have directly participated in the event through commitment of time and labor. (Voila! More volunteers). Additional monies are used for permanent improvements to City parks for all to enjoy.

From 1979 to 1984 the yearly volunteer base of the Festival grew from 50 to 4,000; participating organizations from 15 to 115; manhours contributed increased from a few hundred to 33,000; and yearly distributed monies increased from $5,500 to $250,000.

In the light of these extraordinary facts, the media quotes now took on new meaning. "Gilroy provided an experience to warm the heart" *(San Francisco Examiner)*; "Garlic now gives the town [Gilroy] a certain dignity" *(Wall Street Journal)*; "Enjoy a town being proud of itself and transforming the pungent aroma of garlic into the sweet smell of success" *(The Urban Fair*, U.S. Department HUD), "Garlic Breathes New Life Into Town" *(Washington Post)*. In reality the people of Gilroy have breathed new life into our town. Garlic is simply the product and the Garlic Festival is the vehicle for people to help themselves and each other.

Volunteers, matched to their Festival job by skill level, ability and or willingness eagerly give hours, sometimes all three days of the Festival, to help the charity or organization of their choice. They contribute their time by working manhours for local hospitals, rape crisis and battered women centers, drug abuse prevention, sports and service clubs, rehabilitation centers for the handicapped, libraries, special olympics, youth, school, church, senior citizen and cultural groups as well as for the better known national organizations such as the American Cancer Society, American Heart Association and the American Red Cross.

Monies received from the Garlic Festival are used by 110 local organizations for everything from their operating budgets, to building a playground for handicapped children, to buying sports equipment or classroom materials. But are the dollars the only motivation for helping? The following quotes are the ones we are most proud of—these are from Festival volunteers:

"It is a convergence of good. It is neighbors helping neighbors in a celebration of our community. It is a timely meeting of preparation with opportunity."

Albert Valencia, South County Alternative, Inc.

"The most rewarding and enriching experience is being actively involved in the festival."

Eleanor Villarreal, Hope Rehabilitation

"The togetherness created by everyone working together to create an event we are all proud of is worth so much more than the financial returns."

Richard Imler, Gilroy High School

"The Gilroy Garlic Festival is a beautiful time when community spirit unites and takes precedence over all other activities. We have become closer as a group by working long and hard hours together."

Karen Rizzi, Childrens Home Society

"Other benefits equally important for the kids are the teaching of teamwork, responsibility, accomplishing a task, development of pride . . ."

William Kauffold, Western Homes for Youth

"The Festival is the epitomy of people giving and sharing of themselves for a common cause. There are always more than enough willing volunteers to get the big job done."

Oscar Torres, Jr., Big Brothers / Big Sisters

So in reality it is not only Gilroy's famous garlic but Gilroy's main resource—its people—that guarantees an enjoyable time for all who visit the Festival.

The festival of harvest is, of course, a unifying event as old as civilization itself, but to do it well is the equivalent of staging an opera or anything else that lifts the spirit. In this regard, Gilroy is approaching the first rank.

San Francisco Examiner

The Festival

The festival, which celebrates the end of this year's garlic harvest, really is smalltown Americana at its best.

Keith Muroaka
The (Santa Cruz) *Sentinel*

"The bulbs biggest booster since King Tut."
People Magazine

Whether you appreciate garlic for its flavor, its health aspects or its folklore, you'll want to travel to Gilroy and experience the annual Garlic Festival. Seeing is believing!

The ultimate in summer food fairs, the Garlic Festival features a truly international array of epicurean garlic delights. Gourmet Alley is the heart of this food showcase, where local chefs perform culinary magic over the firepits in full view of spectators. These wizards work wonders with iron skillets the size of bicycle wheels as they toss the flaming calamari or gently saute bright red and green peppers to add to the top sirloin in pepper steak sandwiches. Mouthwatering mountains of garlic bread, tons of scampi swimming in lobster butter sauce, delicate stuffed mushrooms, cauldrons of pasta con pesto and slabs of sirloin basted in garlic marinade all set the high standards for quality and adherence to the garlic theme that prevails throughout the festival.

Eighty additional food booths operated by service clubs, civic and merchant groups offer a breathtaking variety of garlic creations. After sampling the aromatic offerings of the talented townspeople of Gilroy, visitors can cool their palates with the local wines, a cool drink, or garlic ice cream and desserts of local fresh fruits.

Thousands of garlic garlands and braids and the mouthwatering aromas from the outdoor kitchens create the perfect setting for the garlic displays and demonstrations. Merchandise and exhibit booths offer an array of garlic themed articles such as fresh garlic (pee-wees to colossal), garlic braids, wreaths, leis, dry decorative arrangements, all forms of dehydrated and processed garlic (even deodorized), garlic pills, cookbooks and information on garlic uses and its health aspects, folklore, garlic hats, tee shirts, jewelry . . . just let your imagination go! It will probably be there.

And then there is "Art Alley," seventy-five booths of juried fine arts and crafts featuring many original works pertaining to the theme of garlic. Musicians and theatrical groups perform continuously through-out each day of the Festival with the emphasis on family entertainment.

Mr. Gourmet Garlic and Miss Garlic Festival will reign and festival goers will be encouraged to participate in the garlic braiding and the garlic "topping" (a garlic harvesting technique which removes the tops and roots with sharp shears) and to observe The Great Garlic Recipe Cook-off, described in the next section.

But that's not all! There are also events to entertain you if you choose to arrive in the area earlier than the Festival weekend. These events are the Miss Garlic Contest, Love That Garlic Tennis Tournament, Garlic Golf, Garlic Squeeze Barn Dance, Tour De Garlique Garlic Country Bicycle Tour, and the Garlic Gallop 10K run.

Add to these ingredients a generous dash of California small town conviviality, and the result is a recipe for a truly unique summer experience whose savory memories will be with you long after the participants take their garlic braids, cookbooks, and totes full of garliciana home.

People flocked to this little farming community 80 miles south of San Francisco. When the crowds weren't eating, they were singing garlic songs, swapping garlic seeds and recipes . . . buying garlic souvenirs.

Christian Science Monitor

The big doings—
guaranteed to take
your breath away—
will include a Grand
Garlic Cook-off . . .

Signature Magazine

The Gilroy Garlic Festival Recipe Contest

From the beginning, the Garlic Recipe Contest held each year in connection with the Gilroy Garlic Festival was intended to be first and foremost a wonderful adventure in garlic cookery rather than a commercial enterprise. Because the Festival's primary purpose is to support local charities, it was decided to keep the prizes relatively small so that more of the proceeds from the festival could be contributed to charitable organizations. Top prize is only $200, which is extremely small when compared to other national contests. In addition, the entrants who qualify each year for the final cook-off, held during the festival, are expected to pay their own way to Gilroy to be a part of this event and to bring their own pots, pans and ingredients.

One might think that these conditions would discourage entries in the contest, but such is not the case. Nearly 1000 entries pour in every year from garlic lovers throughout the United States who want to share their great garlic cooking discoveries with others who would truly appreciate them.

Contest rules specify that recipes must call for 3 cloves of fresh garlic or the equivalent in dehydrated or processed garlic. Recipes must be original, and only amateur chefs are permitted to enter the contest. When recipes are received at the Festival office, the volunteer committee chairman and committee members sort through the recipes eliminating those which do not meet the specific rules of the contest.

Those recipes which qualify are then sent to a select group of professional home economists in San Francisco who themselves are in the business of developing new recipes for food clients and who understand all the problems related to such endeavors. They carefully read and compare recipes, searching for the unusual technique or combination of ingredients that might make a particular recipe a winner. If there are any questions about a recipe it is prepared exactly as specified by the entrant and then taste-tested to ensure that it qualifies to be in the finals. Once the prejudging is done, the finalists are notified to be sure that they will be able to participate in the cook-off where the winners will be selected.

Judges who serve at the cook-off are always chosen from the professional food world for their knowledge and personal food expertise. Many have judged the most important cooking contests in the country yet all agree that the Garlic Recipe Contest is the most fun. Past years' judges have included:

First Contest, 1979: Shirley Sarvis, free lance food writer and consultant; Anthony Dias Blue, syndicated food and wine critic; Harvey Steiman, *San Francisco Examiner* food editor; Marjorie Rice, food editor of the *San Diego Tribune;* Rita Leinwand, food editor *Bon Appetit Magazine.*

1980: Jane Benet, food editor *San Francisco Chronicle;* Jean Lebbert, staff food editor *Sunset Magazine;* Jeff Morgan, food columnist; Betsy Balsley, food editor *Los Angeles Times;* Mary Phillips, food editor *San Jose Mercury & News.*

1981: Phyllis Hanes, food editor *Christian Science Monitor;* Vern Lanegrasse, syndicated columnist and television personality; Gail Perrin, food editor *Boston Glove;* Dorothy Sorenson, food editor McClatchey Newspapers; Jan Weimer, food editor *Bon Appetit Magazine.*

1982: Carol Haddix, food editor *Chicago Tribune;* Larry Gonick, syndicated food cartoon-columnist; Kit Snedaker, food editor *Los Angeles Herald-Examiner;* Sharon Cadwallader, syndicated food columnist; Jim Neil, fireman chef on TVs *People Are Talking;* Helen Dollaghan, food editor *Denver Post* and Danny Kaye, noted entertainer and film personality as well as accomplished amateur chef.

1983: Marian Burros, food writer *New York Times;* Joe Carcione, syndicated television personality; Maggie Crum, food editor *Contra Costa Times;* Marilyn Hansen, food editor *Family Weekly;* Sharon Sanders, food writer *Chicago Sun-Times;* Jim Neil, fireman chef TV's *People Are Talking.*

1984: Ellen Brown, food editor USA Today; Al Hart, *KCBS Radio Kitchen;* Jackie Olden, *KNX Radio Food Hour;* Lou Pappas, food editor *The Peninsula Times Tribune;* Dian Thomas, the *Today Show.*

All recipes entered in the contest become the property of the Gilroy Garlic Festival Association, and it is with this wonderful collection of recipes that the Garlic Lovers' Cookbook Volume II began.

All of the recipes received each year are filed by category and made available to community members for testing in their own kitchens. Local cooks select recipes at random which they feel will appeal to their families or the more ambitious may choose to have a "garlic party" at which they prepare an entire meal of garlic laced delicacies. Evaluation forms are provided which include information as to number of servings, ease of cooking, ease of obtaining ingredients, clarity of directions, overall evaluation and appeal and most importantly, freelance comments. There's no mistaking comments such as, "Yuck! I wouldn't serve this to my dog" or "My family loved it" or "Our absolute favorite."

Add only the best from these tested recipes to the winners and finalists from previous years and the Garlic Lovers' Cookbook represents a rare collection indeed.

Appetizers/Antipasti

Winner Best Recipe using Most Garlic 1984 Recipe Contest:
MARY FENCL, Forestdale, MA

This is a truly versatile recipe. The puree can be used on cooked vegetables, fish, steaks, salad greens or baked potatoes. You can double the recipe if you want to keep some on hand.

ROASTED GARLIC PUREE DIP

6 large heads fresh garlic (about 72 cloves)
2 pkg. (8 oz. each) cream cheese, at room temperature
4 oz. blue cheese, at room temperature
¾ cup milk
2 tablespoons chopped fresh parsley
Crudites (mixed fresh vegetables, sliced for dipping)

Remove outer covering on garlic. Do not peel or separate the cloves. Place each garlic head on a large square of heavy aluminum foil. Fold up the foil, so the cloves are completely wrapped. Bake for 1 hour at 350 degrees. Remove garlic from oven and cool for 10 minutes. Separate cloves and squeeze cloves to remove cooked garlic. Discard skins. In food processor, mix cheeses, milk and garlic until smooth. Place in serving dish. Sprinkle with parsley. Serve as a dip with crudites for dipping. Makes about 5 cups.

The annual Gilroy Garlic Festival has grown from a small food editors' luncheon into one of America's largest urban fairs.

Family Weekly

Second Prize Winner 1984 Recipe Contest: KATHE HEWITT, La Jolla, CA

This prize winning cook named her recipe to approximate the word "aphrodisiac," because her husband claimed eating it made him amorous. Who knows? Legend attributes garlic with many such tantalizing properties and this dish certainly cast a spell on the judges!

APHRA DE JACQUES

1½ lb. Monterey Jack cheese (7 x 3 inch block)
30 cloves fresh garlic
4 cups peanut oil (more as needed)
1 tablespoon Italian seasoning
3 eggs, beaten
2 cups all-purpose flour
3 cups French bread crumbs*
3 tablespoons chopped fresh parsley
1 small jar Marinara Sauce

Fried Jack Hors d'Oeuvres

Slice cheese into 30 slices about ¼ inch thick. Peel garlic and slice each clove lengthwise into about 6 ovals. Heat oil in deep, heavy saucepan over medium-low heat. Add garlic ovals and simmer 5 to 7 minutes, being careful not to burn or brown cloves. Remove slices as they float to surface and are light brown in color. Drain on paper towel. Reserve oil for cheese. Mince garlic and mix with Italian seasoning. Spread half the cheese slices evenly with garlic mixture. Press remaining cheese slices on each to make 15 bars. Dip flour-coated pieces into egg again, then into bread crumbs mixed with parsley. Be sure to cover sides. Reheat oil to medium-high and fry cheese in oil a few pieces at a time until lightly browned (takes about 2 minutes). Skim particles from oil as they accumulate. Drain cheese on paper towels and keep warm until all are fried. Serve with toothpicks and Marinara Sauce for dipping. Makes about 30 pieces.

*Use day old bread and prepare crumbs in food processor. Dry packaged crumbs may be used but are not as attractive when fried.

Finalist in 1984 Recipe Contest: ROXANNE CHAN, Albany, CA

The garlic filling used to make this appetizer can also be used to stuff cold, cooked artichokes and cold, blanched green peppers or as a topping for cold, sliced meats.

APPETIZER GARLIC PUFFS

1 small head fresh garlic, separated into cloves
Boiling water
½ cup butter
1 cup all-purpose flour
¼ teaspoon salt
4 eggs

Cover garlic cloves with boiling water. Let stand 5 minutes. Drain and peel. Finely mince. In a saucepan, melt butter in 1 cup boiling water. Add garlic, flour and salt all at once. Cook, stirring, until mixture forms a ball. Remove from heat. Cool slightly, then add eggs one at a time, beating after each addition until mixture is smooth. Drop by teaspoonfuls on a greased baking sheet. Bake in 400-degree oven for 10 minutes. Reduce heat to 325 degrees and continue to cook for 20 to 25 minutes or until golden. Remove from oven and cut in half. Cool. Fill with Garlic Filling. Makes about 20 appetizer puffs.

Garlic Filling

1 small head fresh garlic, separated into cloves
Boiling water
2 cups whipped cream (about ½ pint)
1 cup grated Parmesan cheese
1 green onion, finely chopped
2 tablespoons *each* chopped pimento, black olives and roasted almonds

Cover garlic cloves with boiling water. Cook until cloves are soft. Peel and mash. Stir mashed garlic into whipped cream along with remaining ingredients.

Finalist in 1984 Recipe Contest: FERNANDA S. de Luna, Daly City, CA

This is one snack or party treat that will disappear faster than you can refill the bowl. Or you may just be too selfish to share them with others. A true taste sensation for the serious garlic-holic!

PEANUTS AND SLIVERS

2 lb. peanuts, raw, shelled and skinned, about 6 cups (available in health food and nut stores)

6 whole heads fresh garlic, peeled and sliced to make about 2½ cups slivered garlic
Vegetable oil for French frying peanuts and garlic separately
Salt to taste

Place peanuts in wok that has been preheated with oil to medium-high. Make sure there is enough oil in wok to cover peanuts. Stir peanuts constantly, being careful not to burn them. As peanuts begin to brown slightly, lower heat to simmer, continuing to stir, and cook until light golden brown. Drain peanuts well in wire basket and let cool. Place garlic in skillet preheated with 1½ cups vegetable oil until it reaches medium-high. Stir garlic constantly to attain a consistent color and to prevent burning or sticking of garlic. As garlic browns slightly, reduce heat to low and continue to stir and cook until garlic is crisp and light golden brown. Drain garlic in the same manner as peanuts, breaking up any clusters. Cool. Combine peanuts and garlic and salt to taste. Store in airtight containers until ready to devour!

Garlic is always a many splendored thing.

The Denver Post
Denver, Colorado

Finalist in 1982 Recipe Contest: KAREN MAHSHI, Concord, CA

Another two-time finalist in the recipe contest, this creative cook devised a recipe guaranteed to delight garlic lovers everywhere. Whole cloves are cooked inside spicy meat balls, which can be prepared ahead and frozen before baking, to have on hand to prepare for a few drop-in friends or a crowd. If you freeze the unbaked appetizers, do *not* thaw, just add 5 to 10 minutes to the baking time.

TEXAS SURPRISE

50 to 60 cloves fresh garlic, peeled
12 oz. sharp Cheddar cheese
⅓ cup fresh parsley leaves (stems removed)
1 to 2 jalapeno peppers (optional)
6 cloves fresh garlic
6 oz. hot pork sausage
6 oz. mild pork sausage
2¼ cups buttermilk baking mix

Blanch 50 to 60 cloves garlic in boiling water 3 to 4 minutes. Drain and set aside to cool. In food processor fitted with shredding disc, grate cheese. Remove and set aside. Allow cheese and sausage to come to room temperature before mixing. In dry food processor bowl, chop parsley and peppers, if used, using steel blade. Use garlic press or side of wide bladed knife to crush 6 cloves garlic. Add to processor, along with sausages and baking mix. Process until well mixed. Add cheese, and process only until well combined. Shape into 50 to 60 small balls, inserting a whole blanched garlic clove in each. At this point, balls may be frozen for baking at a later time. To bake at once, place balls on ungreased baking sheet. Bake at 325 degrees 20 to 25 minutes or until golden brown. Serve hot as an appetizer, plain or with a bowl of plain yogurt for dipping. Makes 50 to 60 appetizers.

Onward garlic.
**This innocent herb
has staying power.**
Kansas City Star

Regional Winner 1984 Recipe Contest: HELEN MARTY, Phoenix, AZ

This is a variation of the French "beignets" so popular in New Orleans as well as in France. The garlic is included in the rich egg batter. The filling is made with sour cream flavored with Parmesan cheese and oregano. For more garlic flavor, try adding some fresh minced garlic to the filling as well.

GARLIC FRITTERS

10 large cloves fresh garlic
¼ teaspoon salt
6 tablespoons butter
1 cup water
1 cup flour
4 eggs
3 to 4 lb. fat for deep frying
¼ cup sour cream
¼ cup grated Parmesan cheese
   Dash powdered oregano

Chop garlic fine and add salt. Mash into a paste. In saucepan place butter, garlic, and water. Bring to a boil. Add flour, stirring quickly into a mass. Remove from heat. Add eggs, one at a time, being certain to fully incorporate each one. Form the dough into small bite-sized mounds and deep fry at about 370 degrees until golden brown. Drain on a towel. Cut each fritter into two pieces. Mix sour cream, Parmesan and oregano and place ½ teaspoon of mixture on half of each fritter, top with other half.

Makes about 4 dozen tasty hors d'oeuvres or snacks.

Finalist in 1984 Recipe Contest: PATRICK MARKEY, Los Angeles, CA

This garlic appetizer can be held in the refrigerator for up to 10 days. It's especially good for those who enjoy snacking on tart and tangy tidbits.

WHOLE GARLIC APPETIZER

- ½ cup olive oil
- 8 whole heads fresh garlic
- 2 large sweet red onions, quartered
- 1 tablespoon whole peppercorns
- 4 stalks celery, chopped
- 4 medium carrots, sliced
- ¼ teaspoon *each* rosemary, thyme, oregano, marjoram, coriander, basil (fresh if possible)
- ¾ cup white wine vinegar
- ¼ cup dry white wine
- ½ cup water
- 8 to 10 bay leaves
- ½ teaspoon dry mustard
- 1 small can pickled green chiles, about 4 oz.

Heat oil in skillet. Peel outer covering from garlic heads and take a ½ inch slice from top of each head, exposing meat of cloves, but leaving heads intact. Saute garlic, onions, and peppercorns in oil for 3 minutes. Add celery, carrots, rosemary, thyme, oregano, marjoram, coriander and basil. Saute 5 minutes, stirring. Add vinegar, wine, water, bay leaves and dry mustard. Simmer for 10 minutes. Stir in chiles and simmer for 3 minutes. Remove from heat, strain, reserving garlic and 1 cup cooking liquid. Place garlic heads in flat baking dish. Pour reserved liquid over, cover and refrigerate. Serve cold as an appetizer for spreading on French bread rounds or crackers. Also can be eaten plain as a relish course or cloves peeled and mixed in salads. Makes 8 servings.

Oh, that miracle clove! Not only does garlic taste good, it cures baldness and tennis elbow, too.

Laurie Burrows Grad in
Los Angeles Magazine

Finalist in 1984 Recipe Contest: JUDGE STEVEN E. HALPERN, Emeryville, CA

The unusual anise-like flavor of the Pernod used in this recipe helps to create a sauce of intriguing complexity which blends very well with the oysters. An excellent first course for a very special dinner.

OYSTERS GILROY

12 medium cloves fresh garlic, unpeeled
½ ripe avacado
¾ teaspoon salt
⅛ teaspoon black pepper
¹⁄₁₆ teaspoon cayenne pepper
3 tablespoons Pernod
2 tablespoons Worcester-shire
2 tablespoons heavy cream
4 tablespoons melted butter
2 dozen medium-size oysters in half shell
Rock salt

Wrap garlic in aluminum foil and bake in 325-degree oven for ½ hour. Cool to room temperature. Pinch cloves and squeeze out garlic. Add to food processor with remaining ingredients except butter and oysters and process until mixture is thoroughly pureed. Then add butter in slow stream until incorporated into puree. Place oysters in half shell on bed of rock salt in baking pan. Bake at 450 degrees on middle level of oven for 6 minutes. Remove. Cover each oyster with puree and return to oven for 1 minute. Serve with sourdough bread and dry white wine. Makes 4 to 6 appetizer servings.

TOASTED ALMOND CHEESE BALL

An attractive cheese ball, good and garlicky and all the better when it has aged a little.

Recipe contest entry: Nancy Brackmann, Pittsburgh, PA

2 pkg. (8 oz. each) cream cheese, softened
2 cups grated sharp cheese
3 cloves fresh garlic, minced
Dash Tabasco
1 cup slivered almonds
1 tablespoon butter

Combine first 4 ingredients and form into a ball. In skillet, toast almonds in butter until browned. Cool and insert, one by one, into cheese ball. Wrap in foil and allow to ripen in refrigerator for at least 48 hours. May then be frozen, if desired.

Finalist in 1984 Recipe Contest: ROSINA WILSON, Albany, CA

This marvelous hors d'oeuvre is festive, elegant and absolutely a snap to prepare. Serve with a dry California or Italian white wine such as Sauvignon Blanc or Soave. Or serve champagne to heighten the mood of the festivity.

BAKED STUFFED GARLIC CLAMS

- 20 to 30 cloves fresh garlic
- 3 cans (6½ oz. each) chopped clams, drained (about 1½ cups) or the equivalent in steamed, chopped fresh clams
- ¾ cup butter, softened
- 1 tablespoon fresh oregano *or* 1 teaspoon dried
- ⅓ cup frozen or fresh cooked spinach
- ¼ cup sherry
- 1 cup French bread crumbs
- ¼ cup minced parsley
- 2 tablespoons lemon juice
- 2 teaspoons pignoli (pine nuts) or chopped walnuts
- ½ teaspoon salt
- ¼ teaspoon *each* nutmeg, black pepper, and cayenne pepper

Mince or press garlic to make ¾ cup. In large bowl, mix garlic and other ingredients, except garnishes, and spoon generously into clam or scallop shells. Decorate each with a slice of garlic, pignoli and sprinkle of cayenne pepper. Bake at 375 degrees for 25 to 30 minutes until bread crumbs turn golden brown and centers are cooked through. Serve piping hot with lemon wedges. Makes about 8 servings.

Garnishes:
Sliced large fresh garlic cloves, dipped in olive oil, pignoli, cayenne pepper and lemon wedges

Second Prize Winner 1983 Recipe Contest:
LEONARD BRILL, San Francisco, CA

This spiced up recipe for nachos with whole baked garlic cloves for extra flavor had the judges rolling their eyes with delight as they awarded second place to its creator.

WOWCHOS

2 large heads fresh garlic, separated into cloves and peeled
2 tablespoons oil
  Tortilla chips
¼ cup chopped red onion
1 can (4 oz.) chopped green chiles
⅓ cup sliced pimento-stuffed olives (optional)
1½ cups grated pepper Jack cheese
  Chopped cilantro
  Chopped green onion tops

Coat garlic cloves with oil and bake in 375-degree oven for 30 minutes, or until soft and golden. Cover metal baking pan (approximately 9 x 12 inches) with overlapping tortilla chips. Distribute garlic, onion, chiles and olives evenly over the chips. Cover with cheese and bake at 400 degrees for 5 minutes or until cheese melts. Top with cilantro and green onion and serve. Makes about 4 appetizer servings.

STINKY CHEESE

Easy to make, this excellent cheese spread is good to have on hand to stuff celery, spread on crackers, for grilled cheese sandwiches, as a topping for toasty French bread.

Recipe contest entry: Martin T. Quinlan, Woodland, CA

2 lb. sharp Cheddar or Tillamook cheese
1 lb. Monterey Jack cheese
1 can (4 oz.) whole green chiles
1 jar (4 oz.) pimentos
10 to 14 cloves fresh garlic
½ cup dried minced onion
⅛ teaspoon ground pepper
  Garlic powder
¾ cup real mayonnaise
1 cup water (approx.)

Grate all cheese into shallow pan or mixing bowl. Dice chile peppers and pimentos and sprinkle over grated cheese. Press garlic cloves adding both juice and pulp to cheese. Add minced onions and pepper. Generously sprinkle powdered garlic over all. Thoroughly mix together; then add mayonnaise and blend, adding water as needed to attain a smooth mixture. Store in airtight container for at least 2 days before using. Makes about 8 cups.

Finalist in 1983 Recipe Contest: BETTY SHAW, Santee, CA

The best part of this recipe is when all the dip is gone and all that is left is the bread which is soaked in all those delicious ingredients. Just break the bread up and pass it around!

PEOPLE ALWAYS ASK FOR THIS RECIPE PARTY DIP

 1 loaf sheepherders bread
 ¼ lb. butter
 1 bunch green onions, chopped
 12 cloves fresh garlic, minced finely
 8 oz. cream cheese at room temperature
 16 oz. sour cream
 12 oz. Cheddar cheese, grated
 1 can (10 oz.) artichoke hearts, drained and cut into quarters. (Water pack not marinated)
 6 small French rolls, sliced thinly, but not all the way through.

Cut a hole in the top of the bread loaf about 5 inches in diameter. If you wish, make a zigzag pattern to be decorative. Remove soft bread from cut portion and discard. Reserve crust to make top for loaf. Scoop out most of the soft inside portion of the loaf and save for other purposes, such as stuffing or dried bread crumbs. In about 2 tablespoons butter, saute green onions and half the garlic until onions wilt. Do not burn! Cut cream cheese into small chunks; add onions, garlic, sour cream and Cheddar cheese. Mix well. Fold in artichoke hearts. Put all of this mixture into hollowed out bread. Place top on bread and wrap in a double thickness of heavy duty aluminum foil. Bake in 350-degree oven for 1½ to 2 hours. Slice French rolls thinly and butter with remaining butter and garlic. Wrap in foil and bake with big loaf for the last ½ hour. When ready, remove foil and serve, using slices of French rolls to dip out sauce. Makes enough for about 10 to 12 as an appetizer.

Garlic is the king of seasonings.

Donna Segal
Indianapolis Star

AUNTIE PEGGY'S GARLIC SPREAD

Named for a favorite auntie, this creamy, garlic spread is enough for two whole loaves of French bread. Great as a topping for potatoes, pasta and veggies, too!

Recipe contest entry: Denise Domeniconi, San Francisco, CA

6 cloves fresh garlic, peeled
6 green onions
1 pkg. (8 oz.) cream cheese, softened
2 cups shredded Cheddar cheese
2 tablespoons mayonnaise
3 teaspoons soy sauce

In blender or food processor, mince garlic. Add onions and chop finely. Add cream cheese and mix thoroughly. Then add remaining ingredients and process until well blended. Spread on halved loaves of French bread and place under broiler until bubbly.

MUSHROOMS OF THE AUVERGNE

The creator of this recipe recommends that you set the mood for relaxed dining by playing "Songs of the Auvergne" while you put the finishing touches on this do-ahead starter course. The aroma of fresh garlic and the country songs of France are a perfect blend.

Recipe contest entry: Bob Comara, Los Angeles, CA

12 medium mushrooms
3 to 4 tablespoons butter
10 leaves fresh spinach, washed and drained
3 large cloves fresh garlic, minced (about ½ teaspoon)
3 tablespoons grated Parmesan cheese
¼ teaspoon salt
¼ cup dry white wine
2 teaspoons water

Brush mushrooms with damp paper towel to remove surface dirt and remove stems by girdling with a sharp knife. Reserve stems for other use. Place mushroom caps, tops down, in a well-buttered casserole. Blanch spinach in boiling water for 3 minutes, rinse in cold water and drain. Thoroughly combine garlic and butter. Mince spinach and blend with garlic butter. Fill mushroom caps evenly with butter mixture and sprinkle each with Parmesan cheese and salt. Cover with plastic wrap and refrigerate until ready to bake. When ready, heat oven to 300 degrees, add wine and water to bottom of casserole and bake for 20 minutes until mushrooms are cooked but still firm. Makes 12 appetizers.

MUSHROOMS A LA 'RISSA

Mushrooms stuffed with a combination of nutritious ingredients are a favorite of the Mayrons' 3-year-old daughter who even likes them for breakfast and says they are "yummy."

Recipe courtesy of: Cindy Mayron, Gilroy, CA

24 fresh mushrooms (approximately 1 lb.)
1 medium onion, finely chopped
8 tablespoons butter or margarine
4 to 6 cloves garlic, chopped
2 tablespoons soy sauce
1 tablespoon sherry Dash pepper
¾ cup Grape Nuts Cereal
8 oz. Mozzarella cheese, shredded

Remove stems from mushrooms and chop fine. Wipe caps with damp paper towel; set aside. Saute onion in 4 tablespoons butter over medium-high heat until crispy-brown, but not burned. Add 1 tablespoon butter, garlic, stems, 1 tablespoon soy sauce, sherry and pepper. Cook until mushrooms are soft and have changed color. Add Grape Nuts; raise heat to high. Cook, stirring constantly, until moisture is absorbed. Add 1 or 2 tablespoons cereal if needed. Remove from heat and cool. Add cheese and mix thoroughly. Stuff mushroom caps with cooked mixture and place in 9 x 13-inch baking pan. Top each with remaining soy sauce and butter. Bake at 350 degrees for 15 minutes until mushrooms are cooked and cheese is melted. Makes 24 appetizers.

GARLIC-SHRIMP HORS D'OEUVRE

Even those who claim not to like garlic will help themselves to seconds when you offer them this tasty appetizer spread.

Recipe contest entry: Jan Larsen, Kings Beach, CA

2 cups chopped fresh cooked shrimp
4 tablespoons finely chopped fresh garlic
2 tablespoons finely chopped celery
1 teaspoon vinegar
¼ teaspoon white pepper
3 tablespoons real mayonnaise

Combine all ingredients, adjusting mayonnaise if necessary to achieve spreading consistency. Serve on crisp crackers.

GARLIC SQUARES

This baked appetizer will serve about 8 or 10 truly devoted garlic fans.

Recipe contest entry: Catherine A. Peters, San Francisco, CA

1 cup fresh garlic, coarsely chopped
1 cup onions, thinly sliced
¼ cup plus 2 tablespoons butter
2 cups flour
2 teaspoons baking powder
1 teaspoon salt
2 tablespoons finely chopped parsley
1 teaspoon dill
1 cup milk
½ cup sharp Cheddar cheese

Preheat oven to 450 degrees. Gently saute garlic and onions in 2 tablespoons butter about 10 minutes until tender, but not brown. Sift flour, baking powder and salt into mixing bowl. Cut in ¼ cup butter until mixture is crumbly like cornmeal. Add parsley, dill and milk; stir just until evenly moist. Pour into well-greased 8 x 8-inch pan. Spread garlic and onions on top, then cover with cheese. Bake for 25 to 30 minutes. Cool slightly and cut into squares.

THE GREATEST GUACAMOLE OLE!

A few tips from the Chef: If the avocados are not quite ripe, you may chop them very fine and add a few teaspoonfuls of sour cream or mayonnaise to the recipe. Don't omit the cilantro, as its flavor is essential in this recipe. For a fiery taste, use jalapenos, but be sure to wear rubber gloves to protect your hands while preparing them.

Recipe contest entry: Catherine Miller, San Francisco, CA

4 ripe avocados, peeled and seeded
3 cloves fresh garlic, minced
Juice of 1 lime
1 bunch fresh cilantro (coriander), chopped
5 scallions, chopped
5 peperoncini (mild Italian pickled peppers), chopped or 1 to 2 jalapeno peppers, minced
½ teaspoon salt or to taste
¼ teaspoon Tabasco or to taste
2 medium tomatoes, chopped.

Mash avocados, lime juice and garlic together with a fork. Stir in cilantro, scallions, peppers and seasonings. Stir briskly until smooth in texture, then gently stir in chopped tomatoes. Serves 8 to 10 as a dip with chips.

NOTE: This will hold for several days in the refrigerator, but is best when served the same day.

GARLIC-SPINACH SNACKS

Anyone who likes garlic and spinach should really enjoy this recipe. Can also be made ahead and frozen for later use.

Recipe contest entry: Candy Barnhart, Hollywood, CA

2 pkg. (10 oz. each) frozen chopped spinach
4 eggs
1 can (10¾ oz.) cream of mushroom soup
1 large onion, finely chopped
½ cup canned mushroom stems and pieces, drained
¼ cup grated Parmesan cheese
¼ cup Italian bread crumbs
8 cloves fresh garlic, minced
¼ teaspoons *each* ground oregano and dried basil
⅛ teaspoon coarsely ground black pepper

In saucepan, heat spinach in just enough water to cover until completely thawed. Drain well. Beat eggs in large mixing bowl. Add remaining ingredients and spinach and mix well. Turn into a greased 11 x 7 x 1½-inch glass baking dish and bake in a preheated 325-degree oven for 35 minutes or until set to the touch. Serve slightly warm or cold, cut into 1½-inch squares. Makes approximately 36 snacks.

ALL-AMERICAN EGG ROLLS

Chinese egg roll wrappers, Polish sausages and French mustard combine with garlic for an "All-American" appetizer.

Recipe contest entry: Patricia Trinchero, Gilroy, CA

1 quart cooking oil
15 cloves fresh garlic, peeled
½ cup real mayonnaise
½ cup softened cream cheese
2 heaping tablespoons prepared mustard
4 Polish sausages
1 egg
¼ teaspoon milk
8 large egg roll wrappers
   Chopped parsley

Heat oil in frying pan to medium-high, about 350 degrees. Combine garlic, mayonnaise, cheese, and mustard in blender until smooth. Remove from blender. Cut each Polish sausage into two shorter halves and score lengthwise. Beat egg and milk with fork until smooth. Place each sausage half at end of egg roll wrapper, add a dollop of mustard sauce and roll sausage into wrapper, sealing ends with egg mixture. Fry in hot oil until lightly browned on all sides. Garnish with chopped parsley and serve with extra mustard sauce. Makes 8 servings.

PESTO MUSHROOMS

Large cheese-stuffed mushrooms are topped with tangy pesto sauce and baked for 15 minutes, just until all the flavors blend. If fresh basil isn't available, fresh spinach can be substituted.

Recipe contest entry: Jonny Butcher, North Highlands, CA

16 large fresh mushrooms
2 or more oz. feta cheese

Clean mushrooms; remove stems and reserve for other use. Place mushroom caps, hollow side up, on rimmed 10 x 15-inch baking sheet. Fill each cap with feta cheese and set aside.

Pesto
2½ cups lightly packed fresh basil leaves *or* 2½ cups fresh spinach leaves and 3 tablespoons dry basil
5 oz. Parmesan cheese, cut into chunks *or* 1 cup grated Parmesan
3 cloves fresh garlic, peeled
¼ cup shelled walnuts
⅓ cup olive oil, preferably extra virgin

In food processor with metal blade, process basil, Parmesan cheese, garlic and walnuts until thoroughly combined. With processor running, slowly drizzle in oil and continue processing 5 to 10 seconds longer until well mixed. Top stuffed mushroom caps with about 1 tablespoon pesto and bake in preheated oven at 375 degrees for 15 to 20 minutes. Makes 5 to 6 servings.

The soul of pesto may be basil, but its heart is garlic.

Pittsburgh Press

DIP WITH A ZIP

Tone it down or spice it up, but serve this zippy dip with fresh, fried tortilla chips for the best taste. Good with vegetables, too, or spread on a sandwich.

Recipe contest entry: Florence M. Zimmer, El Centro, CA

1 cup sour cream
1 pkg. (3 oz.) cream cheese, softened
5 green onions, finely chopped
4 cloves fresh garlic, minced
3 tablespoons chopped chiles (or to taste)
2 tablespoons salsa (or to taste)
2 jalapeno peppers, seeded and chopped
Salt and pepper to taste

Stir all ingredients together, cover and refrigerate until flavors have blended before serving. Makes 1½ cups.

MEXI-GILROY GARLIC DIP

House Rules: "No socializing or kissing allowed until everyone has tasted this garlicky dip." And it's great for discouraging party crashers. One friendly "Hi-i-i-i" is bound to send them scurrying.

Recipe contest entry: Sylvia Barber, Danville, CA

1 cup small curd cottage cheese
1 cup real mayonnaise
1 can (4 oz.) diced green chiles
1 can (4 oz.) sliced black olives
6 cloves fresh garlic, minced
4 green onions, with tops, finely diced
1 large tomato, finely chopped
Salt and pepper to taste

Mix together all ingredients, cover and refrigerate. Serve with chips or veggies. Makes 4 cups.

GARLIC HERB DIP

This creamy dip can be thinned with ⅔ cup milk or buttermilk to make a delicious salad dressing or add 2 egg yolks and ¼ cup milk and pour over chicken before baking.

Recipe contest entry: Paula Linville, Aloha, OR

1 cup sour cream
½ cup real mayonnaise
4 large cloves fresh garlic, minced
4 full sprigs fresh parsley, finely chopped
2 tablespoons Worcestershire sauce
1 heaping tablespoon finely minced onion
1 tablespoon dill weed
1 teaspoon seasoned salt
3 drops Tabasco (or to taste)

Combine all ingredients thoroughly, cover and refrigerate overnight or up to four days for more potent flavor. Serve with dippers of your choice. Makes about 1½ cups.

FRESH GARLIC VEGETABLE DIP

Although there are vegetables in the dip itself, fresh vegetables for dipping also work well with this single, flavorful and healthful appetizer.

Recipe contest entry: Susan Centrone, Sepulveda, CA

1 carrot, finely chopped
⅓ cup peeled and chopped cucumber
⅓ cup chopped zucchini
2 green onions, finely chopped
1 pkg. (8 oz.) cream cheese, softened
½ cup sour cream or Imo dressing
2 large cloves fresh garlic, minced
½ teaspoon salt
½ teaspoon dill weed
3 drops Tabasco

Combine all ingredients, cover and refrigerate. Good served with wheat crackers. Makes about 2½ cups.

TENNENT GARLIC DIP

The originator of this recipe says it will "knock your socks off it's so good."

Recipe contest entry: Barbara Anderson, Portland, OR

1 carton (16 oz.) small curd cottage cheese
⅓ cup real mayonnaise
6 cloves fresh garlic
Sea salt to taste

Whirl all ingredients in food processor or blender until smooth, cover and refrigerate. Serve with chips. Makes about 1½ cups.

MANNY'S PORTUGUESE GARLIC DIP

Manny says this is soooo garlicky and soooo good that it always receives raves from guests or at potlucks.

Recipe contest entry: Manny Santos, Carmichael, CA

1 pkg. (8 oz.) cream cheese, softened
6 to 8 large cloves fresh garlic, minced (or more for the daring)
¾ to 1 cup real mayonnaise
1 teaspoon Worcestershire sauce (or to taste)
Salt and pepper to taste

Mix all ingredients thoroughly, using just enough mayonnaise to reach preferred spreading or dipping consistency. Serve with chips for dipping or crackers for spreading. Makes 2 cups.

GARLIC VEGGIE DIP

Water chestnuts are a succulent and surprising addition to this easy-to-prepare dip.

Recipe contest entry: Mrs. Milton Falk, Onaga, KS

1 cup sour cream
1 cup real mayonnaise
1 teaspoon instant minced garlic
¼ cup chopped onion
¼ cup chopped parsley
¼ cup chopped water chestnuts

Mix all ingredients together, cover and chill. Serve with fresh crisp vegetables. Makes 2½ cups.

GARLIC ARTICHOKE DIP

Fresh garlic combines with artichokes from nearby Castroville to produce a tasty dip which is equally good with crispy chips, preferably the lower salt varieties, or fresh vegetable dippers. And oh, so easy!

Recipe courtesy of: Barbara Hay, Gilroy, CA

3 cloves fresh garlic, peeled
2 cans (8½ oz. each) artichoke hearts, drained
1 cup grated Parmesan cheese
1 cup real mayonnaise
   Juice of 1 lemon
   Dash of Tabasco
   Fresh vegetables or chips for dipping

In food processor with metal blade, chop garlic and artichoke hearts until medium fine. Place in small baking dish, add remaining ingredients and mix thoroughly. Bake in 350-degree oven for 30 minutes or until golden brown on top. Serve with vegetables or chips for dipping. Makes about 6 servings.

CREAMY GARLIC GUACAMOLE

Don't relegate this garlic lovers' guacamole to the chip and dip department. Use it as a topping for poultry dishes, dolloped into soups, or spread on pita or other breads before adding meat or cheese to make savory sandwiches.

Recipe contest entry: Becky Ayres, Salem, OR

1 large or 2 small heads (not cloves) fresh garlic
1 ripe avocado
1 pkg. (3 oz.) cream cheese, softened
3 tablespoon sour cream
1 tablespoon fresh lemon juice
¼ teaspoon salt

Place whole head(s) of garlic in baking dish, drizzle with oil and roast in 350-degree oven for about 1 hour or until garlic is soft. When cool, gently separate cloves and squeeze garlic out into blender or bowl. Peel and pit avocado, add to garlic along with remaining ingredients. Blend or mash until smooth. Serve with vegetables and chips or as a topping for Mexican dishes. Makes approximately 1½ cups.

DRAGON DIP

This garlic-cheese dip should be served warm in a chafing dish with chips, crackers or, better yet, with fresh vegetables.

Recipe contest entry: Cynthia Kannenberg, Brown Deer, WI

1 pkg. (8 oz.) cream cheese
6 cloves fresh garlic, finely minced *or* 1½ teaspoon garlic powder
2 cups grated Cheddar cheese
6 tablespoons half-and-half
1 teaspoon Worcestershire sauce
¼ teaspoon dry mustard
¼ teaspoon onion salt
3 drops Tabasco
6 slices bacon, fried crisp and crumbled

Mix all ingredients except bacon in top of double boiler. Cook, stirring, until smooth and blended. Add bacon and heat through. Place in chafing dish and serve with dippers of your choice. Makes 3 cups.

Vegetables, Salads and Dressings

Regional Winner 1984 Recipe Contest: DR. JOYCE M. JOHNSON, Atlanta, GA

Onions and garlic are "kissin' cousins" in the plant kingdom with quite different individual flavors which blend together beautifully in this elegant baked vegetable dish.

ONIONS STUFFED WITH GARLIC AND CHESTNUTS

4 large Spanish onions
4 slices bacon, chopped
1 tablespoon butter
1 whole head fresh garlic, peeled and chopped
1 can (8 oz.) water chestnuts, drained and chopped
¼ cup bread crumbs
½ teaspoon salt
¼ teaspoon black pepper
1 cup apple cider

Put the unskinned onions in boiling water for about 5 minutes. Remove and cool. Cut off tops, peel, and scoop out the insides. Chop the insides of onions. Set aside. In frying pan cook bacon until crisp. Drain off fat, add butter and saute the bacon bits, chopped onion, and the chopped cloves of garlic until just lightly brown. Add the water chestnuts and bread crumbs and continue to brown for another 3 minutes. Add salt and pepper. Fill each onion with the mixture. Place in casserole. Pour apple cider over and bake at 375 degrees for 45 to 50 minutes. Makes 4 servings.

EGGPLANT DELIGHT

Originated in 1900 by Elizabeth Powell's grandmother, Elizabeth Shallow Bowden, this highly acclaimed dish has been updated somewhat over the years. It qualifies as a vegetarian dinner and can be doubled to feed a large crowd.

Recipe contest entry: Elizabeth Powell, Media, PA

4 eggplants
4 cloves fresh garlic, peeled
½ lb. *each* shredded Cheddar and Swiss cheeses
3 to 4 tablespoons butter

Lightly spray two 12 x 9 x 2-inch ovenproof casseroles with Pam. Peel and slice eggplant lengthwise about ¼ inch thick. Slice garlic lengthwise in paper thin slices. Arrange layers of eggplant and garlic in casseroles with cheeses and dots of butter separating each, ending with a top layer of garlic and butter. Bake at 375 degrees for about 45 minutes or until deep brown in color, bubbly and crusted. Makes 10 ample servings.

Regional Winner 1982 Recipe Contest   ILENE HELLMAN, Kennett, MO

An Oriental-style dish very good served over rice.

GARLIC EGGPLANT

½ lb. ground pork
2 tablespoons soy sauce
1½ lb. eggplant, peeled and cut into ½ inch squares
1 large onion, chopped
⅓ cup sherry
3 tablespoons oyster sauce
2 teaspoons sesame oil
1 teaspoon sugar
3 tablespoons peanut oil
10 cloves fresh garlic, minced
1 tablespoon chili paste with garlic
½ teaspoon ginger, minced

Mix pork with 1 tablespoon soy sauce in small bowl and set aside. Combine eggplant and onion in another bowl. Mix sherry, oyster sauce, remaining soy sauce, sesame oil and sugar in small bowl and set aside. Heat wok or electric skillet until hot; pour in peanut oil and add minced garlic, chili paste and ginger. Cook for a few seconds, stirring constantly. Add pork mixture and stir fry, stirring constantly, until pork loses pink color. Add eggplant and onion mixture. Stir in sauce, adding more sherry if necessary for liquid to be about halfway up mixture in wok. Cover and cook on high heat for about 7 minutes. If sauce evaporates before eggplant is tender, add more sherry as needed. When eggplant is tender, uncover and cook until most of remaining sauce has evaporated. Serve immediately. Makes 4 servings.

MIDDLE EAST CARROT SALAD

A dish to serve as an accent with meat and potatoes, rice or pasta.

Recipe contest entry: Marion Marshall, Van Nuys, CA

6 large carrots, peeled and cooked
3 or 4 cloves fresh garlic, minced
1 tablespoon salad oil
1 tablespoon paprika
1 tablespoon chopped parsley
1 teaspoon salt
½ teaspoon cumin
Juice of a large lemon *or*
1½ tablespoons vinegar

Slice carrots into ¼ inch rounds. Mix all other ingredients and add to carrots. Marinate 3 to 4 hours or overnight. Makes 4 servings.

Winner 1982 Recipe Contest: ROSINA WILSON, Albany CA

This winning recipe from a very talented lady combines steamed artichokes and whole cloves of garlic which are dipped in a tantalizing basil-laced aioli sauce, then drawn between the teeth to extract the pulp and sauce simultaneously. Thoroughly delightful! The name for the sauce, "Baioli," came from her daughter. It's a contraction of Basil and Aioli. Substitute fresh tarragon for "Taioli," fresh dill for "Daioli," or parsley for "Paioli."

ARTICHOKES ALLA ROSINA

6 medium artichokes
6 large heads fresh garlic
1 large lemon, halved
½ teaspoon salt
½ cup olive oil

Clean artichokes and place in a large kettle. Peel off outer papery skin from garlic, leaving heads intact. Nestle garlic heads among artichokes. Add water to cover artichokes half way, squeeze in juice from lemons, and tuck in the lemon peels. Add salt, and pour olive oil over. Bring to a boil, and simmer 45 to 60 minutes, until tender, depending on size of artichokes. Drain well. Serve warm or cold, with Baioli Sauce. The garlic heads will be soft enough to eat like the artichokes, picking off cloves, pulling out pulp between the teeth, and discarding skin. Makes 6 servings.

⇨

Let's face it, is there a mortal soul who can deny that this cousin of the onion is not one of the most important seasoning agents known to man?

Home Economics Reading Service
Washington, D.C.

Baioli Sauce

4 to 6 cloves fresh garlic, peeled
2 egg yolks
3 tablespoons lemon juice
1 tablespoon Dijon-style mustard
½ teaspoon salt
1 cup olive oil
½ cup fresh basil leaves

In blender jar, place 4 to 6 cloves fresh garlic, peeled, 2 egg yolks, 3 tablespoons lemon juice, 1 tablespoon mustard and ½ teaspoon salt. Cover and blend smooth. With blender running, remove cover and very slowly pour in 1 cup olive oil in a very thin stream. Cover blender, turn off and scrape down sides. Adjust seasoning. Add ½ cup fresh sweet basil leaves, and blend briefly, until coarsely chopped.

NOTE: This variation on the classic French Aioli, can dress up plain meat or fish, raw or cooked vegetables (especially tomatoes), boiled potatoes, hard-cooked or poached eggs, hot or cold soups. Different herbs may be substituted for basil. Use tarragon for Taioli, as sauce for grilled or cold broiled chicken; dill weed for Daioli for fish, especially salmon; fresh parsley for Paioli for a milder flavor. Experiment and enjoy.

SPINACH SALAD

A delicious salad with a good, garlicky bite to it!

Recipe contest entry: Lillie S. Marlork, Vallejo, CA

1 lb. fresh spinach, washed and dried
⅓ cup finely diced sharp Cheddar cheese
⅓ cup finely chopped celery
2 hard-cooked eggs, chopped fine
⅓ cup salad oil
5 cloves fresh garlic, crushed
2 tablespoons *each* lemon juice and vinegar
1 teaspoon sugar
1 teaspoon Dijon-style or brown mustard
½ teaspoon salt
Dash pepper

Cut stems from spinach and tear leaves into large bite-sized pieces. Combine in salad bowl with cheese and celery. Prepare Vinaigrette dressing by combining remaining ingredients in bottle and shaking well. Remove large pieces of garlic and pour dressing over spinach mixture. Toss lightly and refrigerate several hours before serving. Makes 8 servings.

Serve this dish warm or cold, as an hors d'oeuvre or as a main dish lunch. It's delicious no matter how you serve it.

ARTICHOKE PIE

4 or 5 cloves fresh garlic
1 medium onion
2 tablespoons butter
3 large eggs
1 cup whipping cream
½ cup shredded Mozzarella cheese
¼ cup grated Parmesan cheese
Salt and pepper to taste
1 can (8½ oz.) artichoke hearts*
1 unbaked 9-inch pastry shell**

Mince garlic and thinly slice onion. Saute in butter until soft and golden (do not brown). Beat eggs and add cream, cheeses, salt and pepper to taste, and garlic-onion mixture. Drain and cut artichokes in quarters. Add to egg mixture and gently pour into pastry shell. Bake in hot oven (400 degrees) about 45 minutes until set. Serve warm or cold, as entree or appetizer. Makes one 9-inch pie.

*Or use, 1 small package frozen artichoke hearts. Parboil and drain well.

**Use your favorite recipe, or a frozen deep 9-inch shell.

EILEEN'S GREENS

Napa cabbage, also called Chinese cabbage, looks somewhat like a combination of Romaine lettuce and celery, but the individual leaves are pale green at the top and blanched white at the bottom. It is excellent in salads or cooked as a vegetable.

1 tablespoon sesame oil
3 cloves fresh garlic, minced
7 large leaves Napa cabbage, washed and cut in bite-size pieces
¼ onion, chopped
1 tomato, washed and sliced
2 tablespoons soy sauce
1 tablespoon sugar

Heat sesame oil in skillet to 475 degrees. Saute garlic, being careful not to burn. Add cabbage and onion. Stir fry for 1 minute. Add tomato, soy sauce and sugar. Cook for 2 minutes. Makes 4 servings.

Finalist in 1982 Recipe Contest: ALICE GRAY, Berkeley, CA

Long, gentle cooking brings out the flavor of this delicacy, which is prepared here in the Scandinavian manner with yogurt, sour cream and vinegar, laced with the bite of fresh garlic. The cheesecloth sack, by the way, used for holding the garlic is not a necessity, only a convenience for retrieving the cloves for mashing.

SCANDINAVIAN TRIPE SALAD

1 lb. tripe
2 quarts cold water
½ lemon
1 teaspoon salt
4 to 6 cloves fresh garlic, unpeeled
½ cup sour cream
½ cup plain yogurt
2 tablespoons white wine vinegar
1 teaspoon sugar
¼ teaspoon white pepper
Salt to taste
Minced chives

Rinse tripe in cold water, drain, and place in large saucepan with 2 quarts cold water. Squeeze juice from lemon over tripe and drop in the peel. Add salt and bring gently to boil, turn heat to low and simmer until tender, 20 minutes to 2 hours, depending on tripe. Meanwhile, tie garlic cloves in a little cheesecloth sack, drop into kettle and cook until very tender, at least 20 minutes. Remove garlic, cool sufficiently to handle and squeeze the garlic out of its peel into a medium-sized bowl. Add sour cream, yogurt, vinegar, sugar and pepper and mix well. Chill. When tripe is tender, rinse in cold water, drain and cool. Cut into coarse or medium julienne strips and mix with the dressing. Add salt to taste, mound into a serving bowl and chill. At serving time, sprinkle with chopped chives. Serve as an hors d'oeuvre or as the main course of a light lunch. Makes 4 servings.

Nothing beats the versatility of garlic, the great international seasoning.

Betsy Balsley in the
Los Angeles Times

Finalist in the 1982 Recipe Contest: BILL SCALES, Gilroy, CA

Fresh whole tomatoes are scooped out and filled with a savory mixture of onion, sausage, garlic and bread crumbs, then baked with their caps on until juicy and tender.

TOMATOES A LA WILLIAM

6   medium to large tomatoes
Salt
Garlic powder
2   lb. ground sausage meat
2   tablespoons butter
3   onions, diced
4   cloves fresh garlic, minced
⅓   bunch fresh parsley, finely chopped
¼   cup bread crumbs

Cut tops from tomatoes and set aside. Scoop out insides of tomatoes and reserve for another use. Sprinkle insides of tomatoes with salt and garlic powder and turn upside down on paper towels to drain. Brown sausage in buttered skillet. Drain and discard fat. Saute onions and garlic in butter until soft. Combine with sausage, parsley and bread crumbs. Cook gently over medium heat 5 minutes. Spoon into tomato shells and set tops back in place. Sprinkle lightly with additional bread crumbs. Bake uncovered at 325 degrees 45 minutes. Makes 6 servings.

BEST BROCCOLI

Prepare this dish well ahead so that the broccoli can refrigerate long enough to permit the flavors to penetrate. Then serve cold, preferably with a homemade garlic mayonnaise such as Marie's Aioli (page 00).

Recipe contest entry: Sara Janene Evans, San Luis Obispo, CA

1½ lb. fresh broccoli
10 large cloves fresh garlic, unpeeled
⅓   cup red wine vinegar
3   tablespoons olive oil
2   teaspoons salt

Separate broccoli into flowerets with small stems, then peel main trunk and slice into strips. Crush garlic partially, using the flat side of a knife. Fill large pot with water, add all ingredients being sure that broccoli stems are submerged, and cook, covered, until tender. Drain and refrigerate for several hours or overnight. Makes 4 servings.

Regional Winner 1981 Recipe Contest: HARRIETT MACHT, Santa Rosa, CA

Bread may be the staff of life, but potatoes run a close second. You can never have too many good recipes for serving potatoes. This regional contest winner kept her recipe simple, but it is simply delicious.

GARLIC POTATOES WITH CHEESE SAUCE

3 large potatoes
1 medium onion
6 or more large cloves fresh garlic
2 tablespoons butter
½ cup grated Cheddar cheese

Pare and *thinly* slice potatoes; peel and mince onion; peel garlic. Grease a 10-inch baking dish or equivalent-size casserole. Cover bottom with one layer potatoes. Sprinkle with minced onion. Using a garlic press, press 2 cloves garlic and sprinkle over potatoes. Dot with a portion of the butter. Repeat until all potatoes are used, making 3 or 4 layers. Pour Cheese Sauce over potatoes. Sprinkle ½ cup grated cheese over top. Cover and bake in moderate oven (350 degrees) 30 minutes. Uncover and bake 30 minutes longer until potatoes are done. Makes 6 generous servings.

Cheese Sauce
2 tablespoons butter
2 tablespoons flour
½ teaspoon *each* salt and dry mustard
Dash of paprika
¾ cup grated Cheddar cheese
½ cup milk

Melt butter in a saucepan. Blend in flour. Slowly stir in milk. Cook and stir over moderate heat until sauce is smooth and slightly thickened. Blend in salt and dry mustard, a generous dash paprika, and ¾ cup grated Cheddar cheese. Heat, stirring, until cheese melts.

Regional Winner in 1982 Recipe Contest   JIMMY HOBBS, Palacios, TX

Rarely does anyone do anything quite so special with carrots. Prepare them ahead, if you wish, and bake about 20 minutes before serving. The sweetness of the cooked carrot and garlic makes a very happy blend.

GARLIC-CHEESE FILLED CARROTS

1 lb. carrots (6 to 8 large)
1 teaspoon salt
½ teaspoon sugar
3 cloves fresh garlic
1½ cups grated mild Cheddar cheese
1 tablespoon milk
1 teaspoon finely chopped onion
⅛ teaspoon black pepper

Scrub carrots and scrape lightly. Cut in halves crosswise. Barely cover with boiling water, add ½ teaspoon salt and sugar, cover and cook slowly until tender, 10 to 20 minutes, depending on size of carrots. Do not overcook. Drain and cool slightly. Simmer garlic in small amount of boiling water 1 minute. Drain, peel and chop or mash to a pulp. Split each carrot half lengthwise down center. Gently lift out core and mash (or process) to fine pulp, (or process 3 to 4 seconds in food processor). Add ½ cup cheese, mashed garlic, milk, onion, remaining ½ teaspoon salt and pepper and continue mashing or processing to a paste. Mound the mixture into half the carrot pieces and press the corresponding half over filled one. Place sections close together in buttered 8-inch square pan or a decorative shallow casserole. Sprinkle remaining cup cheese over tops of carrots. Bake at 400 degrees 10 to 15 minutes, until tops are lightly toasted. Makes 4 servings.

Cooking with garlic works magic with fresh vegetables.

Nashville Banner

VERY GARLIC ARTICHOKES

Artichokes are wonderful cooked only with fresh garlic for seasoning, but this recipe includes oregano and sherry for an intriguing flavor boost. When she serves them prepared this way, there's nary a leaf left, claims Ms. Van Dam.

Recipe contest entry: Caroline Van Dam, Tarzana, CA

4 medium to large size artichokes 1 head fresh garlic ¼ lb. margarine ½ to ¾ cup dry sherry 1 teaspoon oregano	Steam or boil artichokes until tender; drain and arrange in serving dish, opening leaves slightly. Peel garlic and chop coarsely or cut in thin slices. Saute lightly in margarine, add wine and oregano and bring to a boil. Spoon sauce over artichokes drizzling down through the leaves. Serve hot or cold as an appetizer or a vegetable course. Makes 4 servings.

GARLIC GREEN BEANS

This spicy side dish would be appropriate served with any grilled or roasted meat or fish.

Recipe contest entry: Kathy Borges, Morgan Hill, CA

2 lb. fresh green beans ¼ lb. bacon, diced 1 small onion, chopped 3 cloves fresh garlic, minced ½ green bell pepper, seeded and chopped 1 can (8 oz.) tomato sauce ¾ teaspoon Italian seasoning ½ teaspoon salt ¼ teaspoon pepper	Wash beans, trim and cut into 2-inch pieces. Steam until crisp tender, approximately 7 to 10 minutes. Set aside. Meanwhile, in large saucepan, fry bacon until crisp. Remove from pan with slotted spoon and set aside. Discard all but 3 tablespoons of bacon drippings. Add onion, garlic and green pepper and cook over medium heat until soft, about 5 minutes. Add tomato sauce, seasonings and reserved bacon. Simmer together for about 10 minutes to blend flavors. Add cooked beans and heat through. Makes 6 to 8 servings.

GREEN BEANS AU GARLIC

Served as an antipasto, these good and garlicky beans will get the taste-buds working.

Recipe contest entry: John Proynoff, Phoenix, AZ

2½ lb. young fresh green
   beans
1 large onion, chopped
½ cup salad or olive oil
1 teaspoon paprika
2 tomatoes, chopped
1 head garlic, peeled and
   crushed
2 tablespoons chopped
   parsley
1 teaspoon salt

Wash beans, trim and cut in half if too long. Cook, uncovered, in boiling water, or steam, about 15 minutes until crisp-tender. Do not overcook. Drain and set aside. Meanwhile in separate pan, saute onion in oil until soft, add paprika and cook 1 minute more before adding tomatoes, garlic, parsley and salt. Simmer on low heat for 8 to 10 minutes, stirring occasionally. Add beans and mix well. Refrigerate until ready to serve. Makes 6 to 8 servings.

ITALIAN BROCCOLI

This is an old family recipe which has been enjoyed by the Kovatches for many years. It's an excellent company dish which can be made ahead and heated just before serving. Try it with cauliflower or cabbage, too.

Recipe contest entry: Mrs. A. Kovatch, Sr., River Ridge, LA

1 large bunch broccoli
1 small onion, chopped
8 cloves fresh garlic, peeled
   and chopped
½ cup olive oil
1 cup Italian bread crumbs
¾ cup grated Parmesan
   cheese
1 egg, beaten lightly
   Salt, pepper and garlic
   powder to taste

Steam or boil broccoli until tender. Drain and mash as you would potatoes, leaving small bits of broccoli. In large skillet, saute onion and garlic in oil. When onion begins to brown, add broccoli and stir to mix. Add bread crumbs and cheese and stir until well blended. Remove from heat and add egg. Stir again to blend; add seasonings and stir again. Place in casserole and, when ready to serve, warm in 350-degree oven for about 15 minutes. Makes 6 servings.

CHEESY SPINACH
Easy, economical and very good.

Recipe contest entry: Patricia Lentz, Sunland, CA

1 large bunch spinach or other leafy greens
2 onions, peeled and chopped
3 cloves fresh garlic, peeled and chopped or ½ teaspoon powdered garlic
1 cup cooked brown rice
⅓ cup or more grated cheese
2 tablespoons soy sauce or to taste

Clean spinach leaves well, remove stems and chop leaves and stems separately. In wok or skillet, saute stems, onion and garlic until onions are translucent. Stir in cooked rice well. Lay spinach leaves on top of rice mixture. Cover pan and cook until spinach is wilted. Stir leaves into the rice mixture. Add the cheese and season to taste with soy sauce. Stir until the cheese melts and holds mixture together. Makes about 3 servings.

BIG DADDY'S BIG-ON-FLAVOR SPINACH TREATS
An unusual treatment for spinach. Good for company as it can be made ahead and not cooked until about 30 minutes before serving.

Recipe contest entry: Thomas O. Davis, Waynesboro, MS

2 pkg. (10 oz. *each*) frozen chopped spinach, cooked, drained
10 cloves fresh garlic, finely chopped
3 cups commercial herb stuffing mix
6 eggs
½ cup melted butter or margarine
½ cup grated Parmesan-Romano cheese mixture
1¼ teaspoon salt
¼ teaspoon Tabasco
1 can (10¾ oz.) condensed cream of celery soup

Mix together all ingredients except soup. Shape into small balls. Place in large, ungreased baking pan. Bake, uncovered, at 325 degrees for 20 to 25 minutes. Remove to serving dish. Heat soup to boiling and pour over. Serve hot. Makes 8 to 10 servings.

SPINACH CASSEROLE

The flavor of fresh garlic comes through loud and clear in this vegetable casserole. Look for "Vegeroni" in health food stores if your local supermarket doesn't handle it.

Recipe contest entry: Lila Daoud, Monterey, CA

1 pkg. (8 or 12 oz.) Vegeroni (vegetable macaroni)
1 pkg. (10 oz.) frozen chopped spinach, defrosted
1 container (16 oz.) creamed or Farmer style cottage cheese
1½ to 2 lb. Monterey Jack cheese, shredded
8 large cloves fresh garlic, minced or pressed
½ to ¾ cup milk

Cook macaroni as package directs, drain and cool. Combine with spinach, cottage cheese and Jack cheese and garlic; mix well. Pour into baking pan. Smooth surface with spoon and pour milk over. Bake at 350 degrees for 35 to 40 minutes. Halfway through baking, mix casserole slightly so the top does not get too hard or crisp. Smooth surface and continue baking. Makes 6 to 8 servings.

MEDITERRANEAN RAINBOW

This dish is best served lukewarm with buttered French bread to sop up the sauce. It can be a light lunch, an antipasto or a vegetable accompaniment to a simple (but garlicky) meat or chicken main course. Slightly chilled Beaujolais or a light and fruity Zinfandel would complete the meal.

Recipe contest entry: Rosina Wilson, Albany, CA

1 cup peeled garlic cloves (2 to 4 heads)
½ lb. *each* green and yellow zucchini
2 *each* red and green bell peppers
1 bunch baby carrots
½ cup olive oil
3 small hot chile peppers
1 large onion, thinly sliced
12 wrinkled black olives
4 anchovies, mashed
2 tablespoons lemon peel, cut in strips
Salt and pepper to taste
½ cup chopped parsley
Freshly grated Parmesan

Cut garlic in slivers. Slice zucchini and bell peppers in long, thin strips. Cut larger carrots into quarters or leave whole if really small. In skillet, saute garlic in oil slowly, along with chile peppers, for about 5 minutes. Add onion and bell peppers and saute 5 minutes more. Add zucchini and carrots, stir gently to coat with oil. Cover and steam for 5 minutes, then remove cover, add anchovies, olives and lemon peel. Continue stirring until vegetables are cooked, but still crunchy. Add salt and pepper; stir in parsley and transfer all to serving platter. Top with Parmesan cheese. Makes 6 servings.

NINA'S RATATOUILLE

A delicious, healthful and satisfying dish. Try filling crepes with this mixture and serving as a main dish. If rocambole (a relative of both garlic and shallots) is not available, increase the amount of garlic used.

Recipe contest entry: Nina Landy, Pacific Palisades, CA

1 medium eggplant, peeled and diced
2 to 3 tablespoons sesame oil
2 onions, peeled and sliced
3 shallots, peeled and sliced
3 cloves fresh garlic, minced
3 rocambole, squeezed in garlic press
2 zucchini, sliced
2 medium ripe tomatoes *or* 1 can (16 oz.) drained stewed tomatoes
1 green bell pepper, sliced
1 can (8 oz.) tomato sauce
½ cup dry white wine (optional)
½ teaspoon *each* dried basil and thyme
1 bay leaf
  Salt, pepper and garlic powder to taste
  Chopped fresh parsley
  Freshly grated Parmesan cheese

Salt eggplant lightly and let stand 15 minutes. Dry in paper towel. Heat oil in skillet and saute onions, shallots, garlic and rocambole for 3 minutes until all are soft and onion is transparent. Add eggplant and zucchini and saute for 5 minutes until both are soft and lightly browned. Add all remaining ingredients except parsley and cheese. Cover and continue cooking for about 20 minutes until all vegetables are soft and tender. Garnish with parsley and sprinkle with cheese. Makes 4 servings.

DELICIOUS POTATOES

Another wonderful old family recipe to be shared among garlic lovers.

Recipe contest entry: Pearl Bruce, Winamac, IN

5 cups cooked, diced potatoes
2 cups cottage cheese
1 cup shredded Cheddar cheese
2 teaspoons garlic salt
1 cup sour cream

Mix all ingredients together in order given. Bake at 350 degrees for 1 hour in buttered casserole. Makes 3 servings.

PUREED TURNIPS WITH GARLIC

An excellent flavor combination and especially good with poultry or pork. This dish may be reheated in the top of double boiler.

Recipe contest entry: Kelly Hendleman, Palo Alto, CA

2 lb. turnips, peeled and quartered
12 tablespoons butter or margarine
12 cloves fresh garlic, peeled
Salt and pepper, both red and black, to taste

Parboil turnips 7 minutes in salted water. Drain. Cook turnips and garlic gently in 8 tablespoons butter until both are soft. Puree in food processor or by hand, adding the remaining 4 tablespoons of butter during process. Season to taste with salt and pepper. Makes 5 to 6 servings.

GARLIC JALAPENO POTATOES

Great for a pot luck! The jalapeno cheese adds zesty flavor to "au gratin" potatoes.

Recipe contest entry: Mrs. Milton E. Falk, Onaga, KS

8 medium red potatoes, cooked until tender
1 green bell pepper, slivered
1 jar (4 oz.) pimentos, drained
Salt and pepper to taste
¼ lb. butter
2 tablespoons flour
3 cloves fresh garlic, minced
2 cups milk
2 cups jalapeno cheese, cubed
1½ cups crushed Rice Chex cereal

Peel and slice potatoes. Layer in buttered casserole with bell pepper and pimentos. Salt and pepper each layer to taste. Melt butter in saucepan, add flour and minced garlic and stir until well blended. Gradually add milk, stirring constantly. Add cheese. Stir until cheese melts. Pour over potatoes and top with crushed cereal. Bake for 45 minutes at 350 degrees. Makes 8 to 10 servings.

ROASTED GARLIC POTATOES

A very simple dish with only a few ingredients but lots of good flavor.

Recipe contest entry: Angela Rainero, Oakland, CA

4 large baking potatoes, peeled
4 cloves fresh garlic
6 tablespoons butter
¾ cup grated Parmesan cheese
Salt and pepper to taste

Cut potatoes in half lengthwise, then slice medium thin and place in large bowl. Mince garlic or put through press. Melt butter in a small saucepan and add garlic. Cook on medium heat for 1 minute. Add to potatoes with half the cheese and salt and pepper. Stir until potatoes are well coated. Pour into a greased shallow baking dish. Top with remaining cheese and bake at 400 degrees uncovered until golden brown, about 30 minutes. Do not stir or turn during cooking. Makes 6 servings.

S.O.S. (SUPER OMNIPOTENT SPUDS)

The onion and garlic flavor are surprisingly mild in this light and fluffy potato dish.

Recipe contest entry: Christina Lee, Laguna Hills, CA

8 baking potatoes, peeled and quartered
1 teaspoon salt
1 large onion, peeled and sliced
6 cloves fresh garlic, peeled
½ cup cream or condensed milk
4 tablespoons sweet butter
½ cup grated Cheddar cheese
½ cup buttered bread crumbs

Boil potatoes, onion and garlic in salted water for 15 minutes, or until soft. Drain well. Mash potatoes, onion and garlic until smooth. Add cream and butter and beat well. Place in buttered casserole, sprinkle with mixture of cheese and bread crumbs and bake at 350 degrees for 25 to 30 minutes, until bubbly. Makes 4 to 6 servings.

POTATO-GARLIC PUREE

An excellent accompaniment to roast beef. To prepare garlic puree, place garlic in boiling water and simmer until tender, about 25 minutes. Remove cloves from water and cool. Remove skins and mash with fork to form smooth paste.

Recipe contest entry: Joella Prause Enna, Dallas, TX

4 medium baking potatoes
20 cloves garlic, pureed
3 tablespoons butter
½ to ¾ cup hot milk or cream
½ teaspoon salt
¼ teaspoon white pepper

Peel potatoes and cut into ½ inch cubes. Place in 3-quart saucepan and add water to cover. Simmer until tender, about 25 minutes. Drain well. Mash potatoes until smooth. Add garlic puree, butter and enough hot milk or cream to form a smooth mixture. Whip until fluffy. Add salt and pepper and serve immediately. Makes 4 servings.

SWEET AND SOUR GARLIC VEGETABLES

So easy and tastes just great!

Recipe contest entry: Nancy Stamatis, Union City, CA

2 lb. fresh sliced vegetables (carrots, broccoli, mushrooms, cauliflower, etc.)
4 tablespoons white vinegar
4 tablespoons sugar
1½ teaspoon salt
4 tablespoons vegetable oil
3 cloves fresh garlic, peeled and sliced

Pare, trim and slice vegetables. Combine vinegar, sugar and salt in large jar. Add vegetables and shake to mix well. Cover and refrigerate overnight, shaking occasionally. In another small jar, mix oil and garlic (no need to refrigerate). When ready to serve, drain vegetables and place on a serving platter. Pour garlic oil over and serve with toothpicks. Makes about 4 cups.

TRANSYLVANIAN CARROTS

This dish is absolutely great! It's the garlic that does the trick!

Recipe contest entry: Tracy King, Glendale, CA

1 lb. carrots
6 to 8 cloves fresh garlic
4 or more tablespoons butter
½ teaspoon pepper
Salt and pepper to taste
Chopped fresh parsley

Peel carrots and slice diagonally into 1-inch lengths. Peel garlic and slice thinly lengthwise. Place carrots and garlic in 1½ quart saucepan with enough water to barely cover. Add butter and pepper and cook, covered, over medium heat until carrots are tender. Remove cover and cook over high heat until water has boiled away and carrots are glazed with the butter, about 5 minutes. Salt to taste and garnish with chopped parsley. Makes 4 servings.

ZIPPY ZUCCHINI FRITTERS

Not low in calories, perhaps, but this recipe is another very good way to use the ever-abundant zucchini and who can resist when it's paired with garlic and chiles?

Recipe contest entry: Nancy Bruce, Fair Oaks, CA

2 2½ cups shredded zucchini
4 eggs
1 can (4 oz.) diced green chiles
¾ cup dry bread crumbs
⅓ cup grated Parmesan cheese plus more for garnish
4 cloves fresh garlic, minced
1 teaspoon chicken flavored soup base
¼ teaspoon pepper
Oil for frying

Squeeze as much water as possible from grated zucchini (leaving about 1 cup of zucchini). Place all ingredients, except oil, in a bowl and mix well. Pour oil in skillet to 1/8-inch depth and heat over medium heat. Drop batter into hot oil 1 heaping tablespoon at a time to make 8 fritters. Fry about 5 minutes on one side, turn and fry until golden brown on the other. Sprinkle lightly with additional Parmesan cheese, if desired. Serve immediately. Makes 4 servings.

HEAVEN SCENT

Uncomplicated, but uncommonly good. Zucchini, mushrooms and garlic make this vegetable dish very tasty indeed.

Recipe contest entry: Janice Smith, Delano, CA

2 tablespoons butter or margarine
1 tablespoon olive oil
4 cloves fresh garlic, sliced
1 cup sliced fresh mushrooms
4 or 5 zucchini, sliced thin
1 teaspoon minced parsley
½ teaspoon thyme
Salt and lemon peppr to taste

In large skillet or wok, melt butter over high heat. Add olive oil and garlic and stir for 1 minute. Add mushrooms and stir-fry for 3 minutes. Next add zucchini and stir-cook for 4 minutes. Sprinkle in parsley, thyme, salt and pepper, stir and serve immediately. Makes 4 or 5 servings.

MYRNA'S STUFFED ZUCCHINI

An unusual stuffing for this popular vegetable, it includes both white and garbanzo beans . . . . and garlic, of course. If you cook the beans yourself, be sure to add a bay leaf to the water.

Recipe contest entry: Myrna Slade, San Francisco, CA

6 medium zucchini
1 bay leaf
6 cloves fresh garlic
½ cup chopped onion
¼ cup chopped parsley
2 tablespoons butter or olive oil
1 large tomato, chopped
½ teaspoon *each* thyme,umin and oregano
Dash of cayenne
Salt and pepper to taste
2 cups cooked white beans, drained
1 cup cooked garbanzo beans, drained
2 tablespoons olive oil

Slice zucchini in half lengthwise and simmer in ½ inch water with the bay leaf until tender, about 5 minutes. Cool slightly and scoop out insides, leaving a ½ inch thick shell. Chop insides. Chop 4 cloves garlic coarsely and saute with onion and parsley in butter or oil until golden and soft, about 5 minutes. Stir in tomato and cook 1 minute more. Season with thyme, cumin, oregano, cayenne, salt and pepper. Add chopped zucchini. Mash beans until semi-smooth. Stir into vegetable mixture. Stuff into zucchini shells and place in buttered baking dish. Mince remaining 2 cloves garlic and mix with bread crumbs and olive oil and sprinkle evenly over stuffed zucchini. Bake at 350 degrees for 10 to 15 minutes, until crumbs are golden and crisp and all is heated through. Makes 6 servings.

ZUCCHINI ZAP!

Another delicious approach to preparing the prolific squash, this would be very pleasant served as a light lunch or as a side dish with grilled meats.

Recipe contest entry: Cynthia Kannenberg, Brown Deer, WI

  3 lb. fresh zucchini, sliced
½ cup chopped onion
  6 tablespoons butter, softened
  3 cloves fresh garlic, minced
18 saltine crackers (with salt), crushed
  1 cup grated sharp Cheddar cheese
  2 eggs, beaten
Seasoned salt and freshly ground pepper to taste
Italian seasoned dry bread crumbs
Paprika and fresh parsley sprigs for garnish

Boil zucchini for 20 minutes. Drain and mash. Saute onion in 2 tablespoons butter and add to zucchini with garlic, crackers, cheese, remaining 4 tablespoons butter, eggs and seasonings. Mix well. Pour into greased 9 x 13-inch casserole and sprinkle with bread crumbs. Bake at 350 degrees for 30 minutes. Garnish with paprika and sprigs of parsley. Makes 6 servings.

ZUCCHINI LEAVES

Attractive appearance and excellent flavor are two good reasons to prepare this stuffed zucchini recipe.

Recipe contest entry: Rose Montgomery, Redding, CA

8 fresh zucchini, about 7 inches long
2 cups cottage cheese
2 eggs, well beaten
¼ cup minced parsley
3 cloves fresh garlic, minced
Salt and white pepper to taste
Dash nutmeg
¼ cup grated sharp Cheddar cheese

Cut zucchini in half lengthwise and parboil in boiling salted water for 10 minutes until just tender but not soft. Drain, scoop out centers and discard, turning shells over on paper towels to drain and cool. When cool, place shells in oblong buttered baking dish. Mix remaining ingredients and fill zucchini shells, dividing mixture evenly. Sprinkle each shell with cheese, being careful not to allow cheese to fall between zucchini shells as it will burn. Bake at 350 degrees for 15 or 20 minutes. Makes 8 servings.

ARTICHOKE AND GARLIC FRITTATA

A frittata is nothing more than a flat Italian omelet to which, like the omelet, one can add almost any meat, cheese or ingredient, but always it should be topped with a generous sprinkling of freshly grated Parmesan cheese.

Recipe contest entry: Lisa G. Hanauer, San Francisco, CA

15 to 20 cloves fresh garlic, peeled and coarsely chopped
1 large Bermuda onion, coarsely chopped
¼ cup olive oil
½ lb. fresh mushrooms, sliced
2 jars (6 oz. each) marinated artichoke hearts, drained and halved
8 to 10 eggs
¼ lb. *each* Parmesan, Romano and Mozzarella, freshly grated
⅓ cup Italian bread crumbs
3 tablespoons Italian seasoning
2 tablespoons freshly ground pepper
2 teaspoons salt
Paprika

In large pan, saute garlic and onion in oil until soft. Add mushrooms and saute for 5 minutes more. Add artichoke hearts; let mixture cool. In large mixing bowl, beat eggs. Fold in cheeses, bread crumbs, herbs, pepper and salt. Combine with cooled artichoke and garlic mixture. Pour into two 9-inch cake pans. Sprinkle with paprika and bake at 375-degrees for 40 minutes or until done. Makes 16 servings.

EGGPLANT SALAD TRINIDADELISH

Serve this salad with cold roast chicken, crusty French bread and fresh fruit for a beautiful summer meal.

Recipe contest entry: Thomas Davis, Waynesboro, MI

1 large eggplant
8 oz. shell macaroni, cooked
1 medium tomato, chopped
½ cup olive oil
¼ cup finely chopped garlic
¼ cup freshly squeezed lime juice
4 tablespoons finely chopped parsley
2 tablespoons dry vermouth
1 tablespoon chopped green onion
2 teaspoons seasoned salt
½ teaspoon *each* oregano and basil
¼ teaspoon freshly ground pepper
Lettuce

Wash eggplant; prick skin several times with fork. Place on baking sheet and bake at 350 degrees for 45 minutes or until eggplant is tender. Cool and peel; cut into ½ inch cubes. In large bowl, combine eggplant, macaroni and tomatoes. Prepare dressing by mixing all remaining ingredients and pour over eggplant-macaroni-tomato mixture. Cover and refrigerate overnight. Serve on crisp lettuce leaves. Makes 6 to 8 servings.

SHRIMPLY GARLIC POTATO SALAD

A hot, spicy dressing tops a combination of freshly boiled potatoes and garlic-sauteed shrimp for a new taste experience.

Recipe contest entry: Bob Dixon, Santa Cruz, CA

6 medium potatoes, preferably Red Rose
4 slices bacon, coarsely chopped
½ lb. shrimp, cleaned and deveined
8 cloves fresh garlic, minced
⅓ cup white wine
2 tablespoons brown sugar
¼ cup white wine vinegar
1 tablespoon German mustard
2 green onions, minced
1 dill pickle, chopped
Salt and pepper to taste
Lettuce

Boil potatoes with jackets on for 25 minutes or until tender. Drain. In large skillet, fry bacon until barely cooked, then add shrimp and garlic. Cook, stirring, until shrimp have cooked through, being careful not to burn garlic. Remove bacon and shrimp and set aside. Drain pan and add wine and sugar. Simmer for 1 to 2 minutes. Add vinegar and mustard and simmer for 1 minute longer. Set aside. Slice potatoes with jackets into large bowl. Pour hot liquid over and mix. Add pickle, onion, shrimp, bacon and salt and pepper to taste. Mix well and serve on crisp lettuce leaves. Makes 4 to 6 servings.

LUCIA'S VEGETABLE SALAD

A very colorful salad which is a good, crunchy contrast to Mexican food.

Recipe contest entry: Joyce Childs, Danville, CA

1 cup oil (half salad oil and half olive oil)
⅓ cup wine vinegar
3 cloves fresh garlic, finely minced
2 tablespoons capers (optional)
1 tablespoon finely minced parsley
1 tablespoon Italian seasoning
½ teaspoon salt
Pepper to taste
3 medium zucchini, cut in ½ inch slices
1 can (1 lb.) medium ripe olives, not pitted, drained
1 basket cherry tomatoes
½ lb. whole, small fresh mushrooms
2 or 3 jars (6 oz. each) marinated artichokes, drained
Lettuce

Prepare dressing by combining first 8 ingredients. In large bowl place zucchini, olives, tomatoes and mushrooms and pour marinade over. Refrigerate for 12 hours. Add artichokes and mix. Arrange on bed of lettuce in shallow bowl or platter. Drizzle marinade over. Makes 6 to 8 servings.

EGG SALAD WITH GARLIC DRESSING

For a change, use this egg-garlic dressing on a mixture of vegetables such as green beans, peas, peppers, tomatoes, cucumbers, cauliflower and broccoli.

Recipe contest entry: Betty Caldwell, Danville, IL

6 cloves fresh garlic
1 cup water
8 anchovies, including oil
6 tablespoons olive oil
2 tablespoons vinegar
1 tablespoon capers
3 drops Tabasco or dash cayenne
Salt and pepper to taste
4 hard-cooked eggs
1 lb. watercress or 1 small head lettuce, shredded

Boil garlic in water for 15 minutes until tender. Mash garlic with a fork to make a paste. Chop anchovies and combine in mixing bowl with garlic and all ingredients except eggs and greens. Mix well. Slice eggs in quarters. Tear greens into bite-size pieces and arrange on platter. Top with eggs and pour dressing over. Makes 4 servings.

GARLICKY PASTA CHICKEN SALAD

In this recipe, the large amount of garlic, cooked slowly in rosemary-scented olive oil, develops a rich, exquisite flavor.

Recipe contest entry: Mary Jane Himel, Palo Alto, CA

6 whole heads fresh garlic
¾ cup olive oil
4 rosemary sprigs (optional)
¼ cup fresh basil *or* 2 teaspoons dried
1 tablespoon fresh rosemary leaves *or 1* teaspoon dried
8 oz. corkscrew pasta, cooked and drained
2 cups cooked chicken, cut in strips
½ cup sliced green onion
½ cup freshly grated Parmesan cheese
Salt and pepper to taste
⅔ cup chopped walnuts
Lettuce leaves

Separate cloves of garlic and drop into boiling water for 1 minute. Drain and peel. Place peeled cloves in small saucepan with oil and optional rosemary sprigs. Cook gently, covered, stirring occasionally, for about 25 minutes or until garlic is tender. Discard rosemary sprigs and puree garlic with ½ cup of the olive oil, basil and the rosemary leaves. Place pasta in large bowl and add garlic puree, chicken, onion, Parmesan, salt and pepper. Mix thoroughly. Add more olive oil if needed to moisten salad. Let salad sit for 1 hour at room temperature or refrigerate, returning mixture to room temperature before serving. Toast walnuts in 375-degree oven for 10 minutes. Stir into the salad and serve over crisp, chilled lettuce. Makes 6 servings.

Garlic Goes from Accessory to Star Imagine a world without garlic.
No spaghetti sauce.
No veal parmigiana.
No ratatouille.
No Chinese cooking, Italian cooking, or Greek cooking.
No Fun.

Savannah News

MARIAN'S BEANS

This dish is high in protein, and can be used as a dip or a salad.

Recipe contest entry: Marian Chisholm, Marblehead, MA

4   cups red kidney beans, cooked
2   medium onions, finely chopped
2   medium green bell peppers, finely chopped
½   cup *each* catsup, real mayonnaise and sweet relish
3   cloves fresh garlic, minced
2   teaspoons white horse-radish
¼   teaspoon *each* dry mustard and Worcestershire sauce

Rinse and drain beans. Mix with remaining ingredients. Chill and serve. Makes 8 servings.

GARLICKY GREEN GODDESS MOLD

As a spread for crackers, this molded salad also makes a great appetizer or hors d'oeuvre.

Recipe Contest entry: Julius Wolf, Culver City, CA

2   envelopes plain gelatin
½   cup cold water
1   carton (8 oz.) plain yogurt
1   pint sour cream
¼   cup *each* chopped parsley and chopped green onion
5   cloves fresh garlic, minced
2   tablespoons anchovy paste
1   tablespoon white vinegar
2   teaspoons Dijon-style mustard
½   teaspoon salt
⅛   teaspoon white pepper
1   medium cucumber, finely diced
¼   cup celery, finely sliced
¼   cup toasted, slivered almonds
8   lettuce leaves
8   cherry tomatoes
8   ripe olives

Sprinkle gelatin over water to soften. Stir over low heat until dissolved. Cool slightly. Pour into blender with yogurt, sour cream, parsley, green onion, garlic, anchovy paste, vinegar, mustard, salt and pepper. Process until smooth. Pour into large bowl and fold in cucumber, celery and almonds. Pour mixture into 1½ quart mold which has been rinsed with cold water; chill until firm. Unmold onto lettuce leaves and garnish with tomatoes and olives. Makes 8 servings.

Soups

Regional Winner in 1984 Recipe Contest: CARLA MATESKY, Canton, CT

This chunky chicken broth is enriched with a puree made from a whole head of fresh garlic. What better prescription for good health and good eating?

GARLIC SOUP WITH CHICKEN

1   whole chicken, disjointed
2   carrots, minced
2   stalks celery, minced
1   large whole onion, stuck with 2 cloves
1   whole head fresh garlic broken into unpeeled cloves
    Chopped fresh parsley
    Salt and pepper to taste
10 cloves fresh garlic, peeled
4   tablespoons butter
2   tablespoons flour

Make fresh chicken broth by simmering chicken, carrots, celery, onion, garlic, parsley, salt and pepper in enough water to cover. When chicken is thoroughly cooked, remove it and skim fat from the broth. Simmer broth, reducing it until it is very rich. Remove unpeeled garlic cloves; squeeze cooked garlic from cloves and mash to make puree. Discard skins. In frying pan, saute the 10 peeled cloves in butter. When lightly browned, add flour and small amount of broth and mix with a wire whisk until velvety. Pour this mixture into the remaining broth, add pureed garlic, and stir. Tear chicken into bite-sized pieces and add to the soup. Sprinkle with fresh parsley and serve. Makes approximately 8 servings.

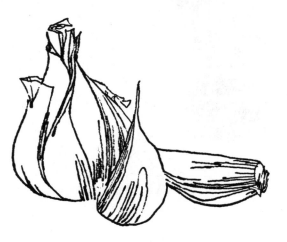

Third Place Winner 1983 Recipe Contest

DEBRA KAUFMAN, South San Francisco, CA

This soup has fabulous flavor, but be sure to serve it with homemade garlic croutons. Use day old sourdough French bread is you have it. Combine ¼ cup olive oil, 1 teaspoon *each* garlic powder and crushed dry parsley, ¾ teaspoon Hungarian paprika and salt and pepper to taste. Cut bread into ½ inch cubes and work garlic-oil mixture into bread. Spread cubes in shallow baking pan and bake at 325 degrees for about 25 minutes. Store in tightly covered container.

CREAMY GARLIC SPINACH SOUP WITH GARLIC CROUTONS

1 large bunch spinach, stalks removed
4 cups chicken broth (preferably homemade)
2 large carrots, grated
1 large onion, chopped
8 cloves fresh garlic, finely chopped
½ cup butter (1 stick)
¼ cup flour
½ cup light cream
½ cup whipping cream
Salt and freshly ground pepper to taste
Sour cream (optional)
Garlic croutons

Chop spinach coarsely. Combine with chicken broth and carrots in 2- to 3-quart pot. Cook 5 to 10 minutes until carrots are tender and spinach wilted. Remove from heat. Meanwhile, saute onion and garlic very gently over low to medium heat in butter, about 20 to 30 minutes. Onions should be very tender and translucent, but garlic should NOT be browned! Add flour and cook, stirring constantly 5 to 10 minutes. Combine spinach/broth and onion/garlic mixtures in food processor or blender in small batches. Puree until smooth. Clean pot and return soup to pot. Add cream, whipping cream and salt and fresh ground pepper to taste. Heat until hot, but not boiling. Garnish with a dollop of sour cream and garlic croutons. Makes 4 servings.

Regional Winner in 1983 Recipe Contest   PEG RHODES, Prescott, AZ

This soup is a nutritious, satisfying, meatless main dish . . . . and it's economical, too. Great served with toasty Italian bread.

ESCAROLE-GARLIC SOUP WITH CHICK PEAS

1   bunch escarole about 1 lb.
4   tablespoons olive oil
5   to 6 medium cloves fresh garlic, finely minced or pressed
1   medium onion, sliced
2   quarts chicken broth (fresh or canned)
2   sprigs fresh parsley, chopped
1   can (16 oz.) chick peas (garbanzos), drained
    Freshly ground black pepper
2   cups cooked rice
    Parmesan cheese, grated

Rinse and drain escarole to remove sand. Cut leaves crosswise into long, thin pieces. Heat olive oil in 4 quart saucepan. Saute escarole, garlic and onions in hot oil for 5 minutes. Add ½ cup of broth, cover and simmer over low heat for 25 to 30 minutes. (The leaves will shrink as they cook). Add more broth if liquid is absorbed too quickly, to avoid burning. Add remaining broth, parsley, chick peas and pepper to taste. Cover and simmer 10 minutes longer. To serve, place ½ cup *hot* rice into soup bowls; pour soup over. Pass Parmesan cheese and enjoy! Makes 4 servings.

CALIFORNIA GARLIC SOUP FONDUE

This recipe offers an excellent way to use up any leftover Champagne. Better yet, open a new bottle and enjoy while you prepare this tasty garlic soup.

Recipe contest entry: Beverly Szabo, Culver City, CA

40 cloves (3 to 4 heads) fresh garlic, minced
3   tablespoons butter
2   cans (10¾ oz. each) chicken broth
2   soup cans water
½   cup extra dry champagne
4   slices French bread
4   slices Gruyere cheese
    Cayenne pepper
    Minced chives

Saute garlic in butter for 10 minutes, stirring often. Do *not* brown. Add broth, water, champagne and simmer 5 minutes. Toast bread. Ladle soup into bowls. Float bread on top of soup, sprinkle with cheese and bake at 475 degrees, uncovered, for 15 minutes. Sprinkle with cayenne and chives. Makes 4 servings.

HUNGARIAN PEASANT SOUP WITH SPAETZLE

This recipe is a family favorite, originally prepared by Helen Headlee's mother. The trick to developing the good flavor is in the slow cooking of the roux. This is a meal in itself and very, very good. Spaetzle are bite-size dumplings.

Recipe contest entry: Helen Headlee, South San Francisco, CA

Soup

2 medium onions, chopped
6 to 8 cloves fresh garlic, minced
6 tablespoons Crisco *or* 4 of Crisco and 2 of bacon drippings
4 tablespoons flour
2 tablespoons Hungarian sweet paprika (Szeged)
3 cups boiling water and 10 cups lukewarm water
1 cup minced parsley
5 to 6 carrots, sliced
4 to 5 potatoes, peeled and cut into large chunks
Salt to taste

Saute onions and garlic in 2 tablespoons melted fat until golden. Drain off excess fat and remove garlic and onion to bowl. Set aside. In same pan, melt remaining 4 tablespoons fat, gradually stirring in the flour and paprika. Continue cooking, stirring constantly, over low heat for 4 to 5 minutes, being careful not to burn. Stir in boiling water and cook for another 3 to 5 minutes. Pour into large kettle filled with remaining water and stir in parsley. Bring to boil, lower heat and add garlic, onions, carrots and potatoes. Lower heat and add garlic, onions, carrots and potatoes. Lower heat, cover, and simmer until vegetables are done and flavors are blended, about 30 minutes. Stir occasionally. Meanwhile prepare dumplings and add to soup when ready to serve. Makes 3 to 10 servings.

Spaetzle

3 cups flour
3 eggs
½ to ¾ cup water
1 teaspoon salt

Stir together all ingredients. Dough will be very sticky. Bring large pot of water to boil and either coarsely grate dough into boiling water or place dough on flat plate and with a sharp knife, scrape and cut off tiny bite-size pieces into the boiling water. When dumplings rise to top, drain and add to soup.

BARROOM CHOWDER

Chowder originated in the New England States. Its popularity is now widely spread. There's a touch of the Southwest in this recipe which gives the soup an unusual and very good flavor.

Recipe contest entry: Barbara Blosser, Alameda, CA

¼ lb. butter
1½ cups chopped onion *or* half leeks and half onion
3 cloves fresh garlic, minced
¾ cup chopped celery, including some leaves
¾ teaspoon *each* cumin (whole seed) and marjoram
⅓ teaspoon sage
⅓ cup flour
3 cups chicken stock or canned broth
2 cups heavy cream
½ cup tequila
6 oz. shredded cheese (Cheddar or Fontina)
2 tablespoons chopped cilantro (coriander)
1 teaspoon red pepper or cayenne
½ teaspoon nutmeg
2 to 3 carrots, half shredded, half cut into ovals
Zest of 2 limes
1 lb. fresh fish, a combination of your choice, cut in chunks

Melt butter in large saucepan over moderate heat. Saute onions and garlic for 5 minutes. Add celery and cook 5 minutes more. Stir in cumin, marjoram and sage. Add flour; stir and cook 3 minutes or until bubbling. Add stock, cream and tequila. Blend. Stir in cheese. Add cilantro, pepper and nutmeg. Mix well. Add carrots, zest of limes. Then add fish and cook until fish is tender, about 10 minutes. Serve with Cheddar cheese-flavored goldfish crackers or warm bread. Makes 3 quarts of soup.

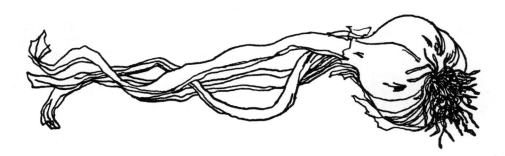

GARLIC-BROCCOLI SOUP

This rich and creamy soup has excellent garlic flavor. It's better the second day around and may be served cold as well as hot. Add a little half-and-half the next day just before serving.

Recipe contest entry: Mrs. Jol Oberly, Memphis, TN

12 cloves fresh garlic
 1 large bunch fresh broccoli
 4 tablespoons unsalted butter
 3 tablespoons flour
 1 teaspoon salt
 ½ teaspoon black pepper
 2 cups milk
 ½ cup chicken broth
    Half-and-half as needed
    Hungarian sweet paprika

Drop unpeeled garlic cloves into boiling water for 1 minute (30 seconds for small cloves); remove from water, peel, and mince. Cut broccoli into buds and stems, discarding woody portions, and cook in boiling water until tender. Remove and drain. Melt butter in 2-quart saucepan. When butter begins to bubble, add garlic, stirring rapidly for a few seconds. Quickly add flour, salt and pepper. Stir constantly for 1 minute. Add milk and chicken broth, stirring briskly with a wire whisk until sauce is thickened. In a blender or food processor, puree broccoli with a little sauce, adding remaining sauce until all broccoli is blended. Correct seasoning to taste and thin with half-and-half to proper consistency. Serve, sprinkled with Hungarian sweet paprika, if desired. Makes 4 to 6 servings.

GARLIC TORTILLA SOUP

This recipe was created by a disabled veteran who obviously enjoys cooking . . . . and eating well.

Recipe contest entry: Mike Conrad, Carson City, NV

15 cloves fresh garlic
 1 cup water
 2 cans (10¾ oz. each) chicken broth
    Juice of 1 lemon
 2 corn tortillas, cut into ½-inch pieces
 2 egg yolks
    Dash of Tabasco
    Pinch of cumin

Peel garlic. In blender thoroughly mix garlic and water. Place in 2-quart saucepan with broth and lemon juice; simmer for 20 minutes. Add tortillas and cook an additional 10 minutes. Remove from heat and cool slightly. Slowly add egg yolks, stirring constantly. Reheat and add Tabasco and cumin. Makes 4 servings.

MEATBALL SOUP, CALIFORNIA STYLE

This recipe is adapted from the popular "Sopa de Albondigas" so popular in Mexico. The Cheese-Butter, added to each serving at the very last moment, could be used to season and enrich almost any clear soup.

Recipe contest entry: Fresh Garlic Association

4   large cloves fresh garlic
½   lb. ground beef
1   large egg, beaten
1½   teaspoons salt
2   tablespoons uncooked rice
¼   cup finely chopped parsley
½   cup chopped onion
1   tablespoon oil
½   teaspoon lemon pepper seasoning
2   cans (10½ oz. each; beef broth
2   cups water
1   cup carrots, cut in 2 x ¼ inch strips
1   cup celery, cut in 2 x ¼ inch strips
1   can (8¾ oz.) garbanzos, undrained
1   can (1 lb.) stewed tomatoes
    Cheese-Butter (recipe below)

Peel garlic. Mash, or put through garlic press, 1 clove garlic. Combine with beef, egg, ½ teaspoon salt, rice and 2 tablespoons parsley. Shape mixture into 20 small meatballs and set aside. Chop remaining 3 cloves garlic or mash. Cook garlic with onion in oil, over medium heat until soft but not browned in covered 3-quart saucepan. Add remaining 1 teaspoon salt, lemon-pepper seasoning, broth, water, carrots and celery. Bring to boiling. Drop in meat balls and simmer 20 minutes. Add undrained garbanzos, tomatoes and remaining chopped parsley. Continue cooking 10 minutes longer. Ladle into large soup bowls and serve with a spoonful of Cheese-Butter. Makes 4 entree servings.

Cheese-Butter
½   cup butter, softened
½   teaspoon pressed fresh garlic
2   tablespoons grated Parmesan cheese
1   tablespoon minced parsley

Blend all ingredients together. Makes about ½ cup.

CREAM OF ARTICHOKE SOUP

This creamy soup depends partly for its seasoning on the herbs and spices in the marinade used on the artichoke hearts. Fresh garlic and onion provide just the right additional flavor balance. A lovely starter course for an elegant dinner.

Recipe contest entry: Fresh Garlic Association

1 jar (6 oz.) marinated
   artichoke hearts
3 or more large cloves fresh
   garlic
½ cup chopped onion
2 tablespoons flour
2 cans (10¾ oz. each)
   chicken broth
1 cup half-and-half
   Finely chopped parsley

Drain marinade from artichoke hearts into 2-quart saucepan. Crush garlic with press or mince and add to marinade. Add onion and cook, covered, 10 minutes over low heat. Blend in flour. Slowly stir in 1 can broth and heat to boiling, stirring. Boil 1 minute or until mixture thickens. Turn artichoke hearts into blender or food processor and add hot mixture, blending until smooth. Strain into saucepan; add remaining can of broth and half-and-half. Heat just to serving temperature; do not boil. Sprinkle each serving with parsley. Makes 4 servings, about 1⅓ cup each.

Garlic is a habit
and a passion.

Kim Upton
Chicago Sun Times

Breads and Pasta

First Place Winner in 1983 Recipe Contest: NEIL MAHONY, Ventura, CA

This recipe is one of the all-time favorite prize-winners. An unusual and outstanding dish. The Mahonys recommend keeping a bottle of olive oil in the refrigerator to which have been added 4 to 5 heads of peeled garlic. That way you'll have it ready when you want to make Bruschetta or you can add lemon juice for a salad dressing, to prepare oysters and linguine or to add to pasta water for flavor and to prevent boilover.

MAHONY'S BRUSCHETTA

1 loaf French or Italian bread without seeds (day-old bread works fine)
10 large cloves fresh garlic, peeled
¾ cup olive oil, preferably extra virgin
1½ cups whipping cream
½ cup grated Locatelli cheese (hard Romano cheese)
½ cup grated Parmesan cheese, preferably imported Italian
3 tablespoons butter
1 tablespoon chopped parsley
Paprika

Cut bread diagonally in 1-inch slices, without cutting through bottom crust. In food processor or blender, chop garlic fine with steel blade and add olive oil with processor running to make a thin paste. Slather garlic paste on cut surfaces and on top and side crusts of bread. Place in 350-degree oven, directly on rack (with pan on shelf below to catch drippings), and bake for 10 to 12 minutes, until top is crispy looking. While bread is in oven, heat whipping cream in heavy saucepan. Do not boil. Stir in cheeses slowly so that sauce is absolutely smooth (a wire whip works well for this). Stir in butter and keep sauce warm until bread is ready. Wait until everyone is seated at the table. Then place crispy bread in a warmed, shallow serving dish with sides. Finish cutting through bottom crust and pour sauce over. Sprinkle with parsley and paprika and serve IMMEDIATELY. This dish cools very quickly. Makes 6 servings.

NOTE: Each guest should be provided with a small saucer for the Bruschetta, as it is best eaten with a knife and fork.

Best Recipe Using Most Garlic 1983 Recipe Contest:

KELLEE KATZMAN, North Hollywood, CA

For those who like to make their own pasta and who love garlic, here is an irresistible recipe for ravioli.

GARLIC RAVIOLI

 5 large heads fresh garlic
 2 cups chicken broth
   (preferably homemade)
11 tablespoons unsalted
   butter
1½ cups ricotta cheese
 1 cup grated Parmesan
   cheese
 1 teaspoon garlic salt
 2 sheets homemade pasta
   (about 5 x 24 inches each)
 1 egg, slightly beaten
⅓ cup heavy cream
½ cup grated Romano
   Cheese

Put heads of garlic in shallow baking pan; pour chicken broth over and dot each head with 1 tablespoon butter. Cover and bake for 45 minutes, or until tender. Strain and reserve ⅓ cup liquid. Allow garlic to cool; then squeeze each clove into a bowl. Discard skins. Add ricotta. ½ cup Parmesan and garlic salt and mix thoroughly. Brush 1 sheet of pasta with egg and place garlic/cheese mixture on pasta in mounds (1 teaspoon each) about 2 inches apart. Place second sheet of pasta over the first and press with fingers around each mound. With fluted pastry wheel, cut up into 2-inch square ravioli. Refrigerate for 30 minutes. Bring large pot of water to boil. Just before water boils, start sauce. In frying pan, melt remaining 6 tablespoons butter, add cream and reduce slightly. Add reserved ⅓ cup liquid and reduce to good sauce consistency. When water reaches a rapid boil, drop ravioli in and boil for 3 to 5 minutes. Remove with slotted spoon and put directly into reduced sauce. Sprinkle with remaining Parmesan and Romano cheeses. Serves 4 to 6 as an appetizer.

Garlic: from Dracula to pasta, herb reeks of history.

Hackensack Record

Regional Winner 1984 Recipe Contest: GLEN PETERSON, Omaha, NE

This sensational and savory garlic bread is made with thawed frozen white bread dough. It's quick and easy and attractive to serve. If you prefer, you can bake it in two 9 x 6-inch loaf pans rather than the Bundt pan.

GARLIC CLOVE BREAD

2   loaves frozen white bread dough, thawed
⅓   cup butter, melted and cooled to lukewarm
¼   teaspoon basil
2   tablespoons chopped parsley
1   small onion, chopped
5   cloves fresh garlic, minced

Cut or snip off pieces of dough about the size of an English walnut. Place into a greased 10-inch Bundt pan. Combine the melted butter, basil, chopped parsley, onions, and minced garlic. Pour over dough. Cover and let rise until double in size (about 1½ hours). Bake in 375-degree oven until golden brown (about 30 to 35 minutes). Cool in pan for 10 minutes and then remove from pan and serve.

Finalist in 1983 Recipe Contest: DIANE TARANGO, Hacienda Heights, CA

A very simple dish but very, very good. Might need more garlic for some. Be sure the Brie is well ripened, so that it will have good flavor.

HOT BRIE PASTA ALA DIANE

1   lb. ripe French Brie
½   cup olive oil
1   cup fresh basil, cut into strips
4   large cloves fresh garlic, minced
4   tomatoes, seeded and cubed
½   teaspoon salt
¾   teaspoon freshly ground pepper
1   lb. linguine or capelli d'angelo (angel hair) pasta
6   oz. Parmesan, freshly grated

Remove rind from cheese and cut into irregular pieces. Combine with next 6 ingredients in large bowl and let stand for 2 hours at room temperature. Cook pasta *al dente* and drain. Toss hot pasta with Brie mixture. Top with Parmesan cheese and serve at once. Delicious! Makes 4 to 6 servings.

Finalist in 1982 Recipe Contest: PATRICIA BISSINGER, Livermore, CA

This bread recipe is from a second time finalist in the Recipe Contest, a very creative cook whose entry won high praise from all who sampled it. It is also excellent cold. "Enjoy! Enjoy!," said Ms. Bissinger, and we did, we did!

KRUSTY GARLIC KUCHEN

Dough:
- 1 envelope active dry yeast
- 1½ cups warm water
- 3 cups unbleached flour
- 1 cup whole wheat flour
- ¼ cup grated Parmesan cheese
- 1 egg, lightly beaten
- 2 tablespoon vegetable oil
- 1 teaspoon garlic salt

Sprinkle yeast over warm water and let stand until bubbly. Meanwhile, measure all remaining dough ingredients into food processor bowl. Add yeast mixture and process just until dough forms a ball. Turn out onto floured surface and knead until dough is soft and no longer sticky. Shape into a ball, place in greased bowl, cover and let rise in warm place while preparing topping.

Garlic Topping
- 1 head fresh garlic, minced (10 to 12 cloves)
- 2 tablespoons vegetable oil
- 1 cup sour cream
- 2 eggs, lightly beaten
- ½ teaspoon salt
- Minced chives *or* green scallion tops

Peel and mince garlic cloves. Saute 3 to 5 minutes in oil over low heat, until soft but not browned. Remove from heat and cool slightly, then combine with sour cream, eggs and salt.

Press dough into bottom and up sides of greased 10 x 15 x 1-inch pan, forming rim around edges. Crimp edge (*or* cut rim to decorate edge). Spread Garlic Topping evenly into pan and sprinkle with minced chives. Bake at 400 degrees 20 to 24 minutes until edges are well browned, and creamy garlic topping is light golden. Serve slightly warm, cut into strips as bread or appetizer. Makes 8 to 10 servings.

Finalist in 1982 Recipe Contest: RITA PHISTER, Riverside, CA

The chile, garlic and Cheddar filling in this braided bread is the surprise ingredient that brought this contestant to the finals in the 1982 Gilroy Garlic Recipe Contest.

SOUTHERN CALIFORNIA'S
BEST BREAD IN THE WEST

1 envelope active dry yeast
¼ cup warm water
½ cup milk
2 eggs
¼ cup soft butter or margarine
3 tablespoons sugar
1½ teaspoons salt
1½ teaspoons ground comino
3½ cups all-purpose flour
   Green Chile Filling (recipe below)
½ cup grated Cheddar cheese

In large bowl of electric mixer, dissolve yeast in warm water. Blend in milk, eggs, butter, sugar, salt and comino. Blend in 2 cups flour, 1 cup at a time. Beat on medium speed of mixer 3 minutes, scraping bowl often. With heavy duty mixer (*or* with wooden spoon) blend in remaining flour to make a soft dough. Turn out onto floured board, and knead until smooth, 5 to 10 minutes. Place in greased bowl, turn over, and cover. Let rise in warm place until doubled, about 1½ hours. Meanwhile, prepare Green Chile Filling. When dough has risen, punch down and turn out onto floured board. Roll to a 9 x 30-inch rectangle. Crumble filling over dough to within 1 inch of edges. Starting from long side, roll up tightly. Moisten edge with water and pinch together firmly to seal. Using a floured sharp knife, cut roll lengthwise in halves. Carefully turn cut sides up. Loosely twist the two strips together, keeping cut sides up. Transfer to greased and floured baking sheet, and shape to 10-inch circle. Pinch ends firmly together. Let rise in warm place, uncovered, until puffy looking, about 45 to 60 minutes. Bake at 375 degrees 15 minutes. Sprinkle with ½ cup Cheddar cheese and bake 5 minutes longer, until browned. Makes 1 10-inch twist.

⇨

Green Chile Filling
  1 large onion, chopped
  8 cloves fresh garlic, chopped
  1 tablespoon butter
  2 cups grated Cheddar cheese
  1 can (7 oz.) diced green chiles

Saute onion and garlic in butter until soft but not browned. Cool. Mix in 2 cups Cheddar and chiles. Cover and chill.

Second Place Winner 1982 Recipe Contest: BYRON RUDY, Livermore Ca

A zesty calamari sauce using two heads of fresh garlic tops this rich creamy fettucine concoction. It was good enough to win second place for the chef who created it in the Third Annual Gilroy Garlic Recipe Contest.

FETTUCCINE GARLI-MARI

  2 heads fresh garlic, about 30 cloves
  2 lbs. calamari
  4½ tablespoons butter
  1 tablespoon olive oil
  ¼ cup packed finely chopped parsley
  2 tablespoons dry white table wine
  12 oz. fettuccine
  ½ cup heavy cream
  2½ oz. freshly grated Parmesan cheese

Put garlic cloves through press. Clean calamari, filet and cut into ¼ inch strips. Saute garlic in 1½ tablespoons butter and olive oil, stirring often, until soft and golden. Add calamari and cook over medium low heat, turning often, until strips curl. Reduce heat, add wine and parsley, and cook 2 minutes longer. Meanwhile, cook fettuccine as package directs (coordinate cooking time with calamari, so both are done at once); drain. Melt remaining 3 tablespoons butter in a hot serving bowl, combine butter, heavy cream and Parmesan cheese, and mix together. Add fettuccine and calamari, and mix together with pasta forks. Serve immediately on warm serving plates. Makes 6 servings.

Honorable Mention 1983 Recipe Contest: ROBERT J. DYER, Gilroy, CA

This Honorable Mention winner went on the next year to win Third Prize with another pasta recipe. This dish will serve 6 or more as a small appetizer or starter course.

FETTUCCINE ROBERTO

1   lb. fettuccine noodles
½   cup oil
¼   lb. butter
24 cloves fresh garlic, chopped
1   lb. fresh jumbo shrimp, butterflied
1   cup chopped fresh parsley
2   cups chopped fresh mushrooms
1   cup chopped green onions
1   tablespoon red pepper
2   tablespoons flour
½   cup dry white wine
1   pint heavy cream
1   small wedge (about 5 oz.) Parmesan cheese, grated
    Salt to taste

Cook noodles according to package directions in boiling water with oil. While noodles are cooking, melt butter in large skillet over medium-high heat. Add chopped garlic and shrimp; cook until shrimp turn pink, but do not allow garlic to turn brown. Add parsley, mushrooms, onions and red pepper; saute for 1 minute. Add flour, mix thoroughly and add wine. Simmer for about 30 seconds, then add cream and heat through. Drain noodles and add to sauce with half the grated cheese. Fold in gently until noodles are well coated and cheese is melted. Salt lightly. If sauce is too thin, continue heating until sauce reduces to a creamy consistency. If sauce is too thick, add cream. Garnish with chopped parsley and additional grated cheese and serve immediately. Makes 4 servings.

There are many miracles in the world to be celebrated and, for me, garlic is among the most deserving.

Professor Leo Buscaglia

Third Prize Winner 1984 Recipe Contest: ROBERT J. DYER, Gilroy, CA

"If you live in the Garlic Capital of the World, it's only fitting that you should be a good garlic cook," claims Bob Dyer, Gilroy businessman, who was also chairman of the very first Garlic Festival in 1979. Bob's colorful spaghetti dish attracted the judges with its stir-fried vegetables, succulent prawns and plenty of garlic — 24 cloves in all.

SPAGHETTACCINI CAROLINI

1	lb. spaghetti noodles
4	tablespoons oil
¼	lb. butter
24	cloves fresh garlic, peeled and chopped
1	lb. fresh jumbo shrimp, peeled and butterflied
1	red bell pepper, thinly sliced
1	bunch broccoli, cut into serving size spears
2	cups chopped fresh mushrooms
1	cup chopped fresh parsley
1	cup chopped green onions
1	tablespoon dried red pepper
2	tablespoons flour
½	cup dry white wine
1	pint heavy cream
1	small wedge (about 3 oz.) Parmesan cheese, grated Salt to taste

Cook noodles according to package directions in boiling water with 2 tablespoons oil. Meanwhile, melt butter in large skillet over medium high heat. Add chopped garlic and shrimp; cook until shrimp turn pink, but do not allow garlic to brown. Set aside. In another skillet, over medium-high heat, stir-fry red bell pepper and broccoli in remaining 2 tablespoons oil. Cook until crisp-tender. Drain and set aside. Add mushrooms, half the parsley, onions and red pepper to garlic and shrimp; saute for one minute. Add flour, mix thoroughly, and add wine. Simmer for about 30 seconds, then add cream and heat through, stirring. Drain noodles and add to sauce with half the grated cheese. Toss gently until noodles are well coated and cheese is melted. Salt lightly. If sauce is too thin, continue heating until sauce reduces to a creamy consistency. If sauce is too thick, add cream. Gently toss in the stir-fried vegetables. Garnish with remaining chopped parsley and grated cheese and serve immediately. Makes 8 servings.

MAMMA'S SFEENJUNEE

Frank, Josephine and Merrie Jo Fees, who entered their mother's recipe in the Garlic Recipe Contest, described this bread as easy, filling, and wonderfully aromatic . . . . and healthful! Mamma even stuck whole cloves into the dough.

Recipe contest entry: The Fees Family, Honolulu, HI

1⅓ cups very warm water
1 envelope yeast
1 teaspoon sugar
3 tablespoons olive oil
4 cups flour
1 teaspoon salt
1 lb. Italian sausage (or Polish sausage, ham or cooked pork)
4 or 5 cloves fresh garlic
½ teaspoon Italian seasoning or oregano
½ cup black olives

Pour water into large bowl, sprinkle yeast over, add sugar and allow to sit for a few minutes while it bubbles. Stir in 2 tablespoons olive oil. Combine flour and salt and add to yeast. Mix well. Knead for about 10 minutes, cover and set in warm place to rise for 1 to 1½ hours. Meanwhile, remove skin from sausage and fry until cooked and crumbly. Drain off grease. Cut each garlic clove lengthwise into 6 slivers. Place in cup and cover with remaining 1 tablespoon oil and seasoning. Cut olives in two and add to sausage. When dough has risen, pat into a greased 9 x 9 x 2-inch pan and evenly sprinkle the garlic-oil over. Force sausage mixture down into dough 1 teaspoon at a time. Bake at 375 degrees for 25 minutes or until golden. Makes 8 to 10 servings.

It can be gentle, alluring and enticing, giving a marvelous subtle flavor to various dishes—a superb herb.

Marie Ryckman
Cincinnati Enquirer

GARLIC FOCACCIA

Northern Italy's answer to "pizza," this "cake which is not sweet" has many variations. To the basic Focaccia add artichoke hearts, preserved sweet red peppers, olives, mushrooms, cheese or anchovies. Delicious hot from the oven, it also keeps well.

Recipe contest entry: Carolyn Ragsdale, Paso Robles, CA

½ cup chopped fresh garlic
⅓ cup olive oil
3 cups biscuit mix
1 cup milk or buttermilk
½ cup grated Parmesan cheese

Gently saute garlic in oil until yellow, about 10 minutes. Pour through strainer and reserve both garlic and oil separately. Combine biscuit mix, garlic and milk. Pour a generous third of the oil into a 7 x 11-inch baking dish or pan. Spread the oil around to cover the dish. Turn dough into dish, pat out evenly with floured fingers. Poke holes into dough every 2 inches with a tool such as a pointed knife blade or wooden skewer to make small holes. Pour remaining oil over top of dough and spread evenly with the fingers. Sprinkle Parmesan over the top and bake at 400 degrees for 24 minutes. Makes 8 to 10 servings.

NOTE: For stronger garlic flavor, do not cook garlic. Add to the dough raw and bake as usual.

There's no such thing as a little garlic.

San Diego *Union*

HOBO BREAD

This bread is baked in a coffee can. It's terrific with stew, and good reheated later. Slice into rounds and pop into the toaster—that is, IF there are any leftovers.

Recipe contest entry: Jacqueline McComas, Frazer, PA

Butter to grease 2 1-lb. coffee cans
4 cups self-rising flour
½ cup grated Cheddar cheese
1 tablespoon dry basil *or* 2 tablespoons fresh basil
¼ cup butter
½ cup finely chopped fresh parsley
3 or 4 cloves fresh garlic, chopped
2 tablespoons honey
2 tablespoons chopped chives
½ cup milk
1 can (12 oz.) beer

Generously butter cans. In mixing bowl, combine flour, cheese and basil. In saucepan, heat butter, parsley, garlic, honey and chives until butter melts. Remove from heat and add milk. Add beer and IMMEDIATELY add to dry ingredients. Combine gently ONLY until moistened. Divide dough evenly into the cans and bake at 350 degrees for 30 to 40 minutes or until tops are very brown. Slice into rounds and serve with plenty of butter. Makes 2 loaves.

PESTO LASAGNA FIRENZA

Pasta and pesto are natural go-togethers and especially good when combined in this delightfully different lasagna. For a good pesto recipe, see Pesto Mushrooms (page 27).

Recipe contest entry: Florence Oefinger, Novato, CA

6 or 7 lasagna noodles
2 cups pesto, freshly made or frozen
½ cup half-and-half
4 large cloves fresh garlic, minced
2 tablespoons olive oil
1 tablespoon softened butter
1 lb. Monterey Jack cheese, grated
3 tablespoons grated Parmesan cheese

Boil noodles as package directs. Rinse in cold water and drain. Mix pesto, half-and-half, garlic, oil and butter in small bowl. Grease a loaf pan and spread several spoonsful of pesto mixture over bottom. Cut noodles to fit pan and place in single layer over pesto. Spread ⅓ of pesto on top and sprinkle with ⅓ of Jack cheese. Repeat twice, ending with cheese. Sprinkle with Parmesan and bake at 350 degrees for 45 minutes. Makes 2 or 3 servings.

NANCY AND J.R.'S PASTA

A crowd-pleasing pasta recipe that can be made with mild or super hot Italian sausage as your taste dictates.

Recipe contest entry: Nancy Mertesdorf and Jeanette Renouf, San Jose, CA

1   lb. hot Italian sausage
2   tablespoons oil
¾   lb. fresh mushrooms, sliced
8   to 10 large cloves fresh garlic, minced
2   medium green bell peppers, julienned
1   bunch green onions, chopped
¼   cup dry white wine
4   tablespoons butter, softened
¾   lb. fresh, thin, coiled spaghetti
6   oz. Parmesan cheese, freshly grated

Remove casing from sausage. Crumble and fry in small skillet. Drain off excess fat and set aside. Heat oil in large skillet or wok. Add mushrooms, half the garlic, peppers, onions and wine. Stir fry until crisp-tender. Meanwhile add remaining minced garlic to butter and set aside. Cook pasta for 4 to 5 minutes or until tender. Drain well. Toss with garlic butter and Parmesan cheese, saving some for garnish. Add sausage and vegetable mixture to pasta and toss well. Makes 12 servings.

LINGUINE CONTESSA

Served as a main course or side dish, this pasta is superb!

Recipe contest entry: Donna Richard, Bala Cynwyd, PA

3   chicken bouillon cubes
1½ cups water
¼   cup olive oil
1   lb. fresh mushrooms, sliced
¼   to ½ lb. prosciutto (thin-sliced Italian ham), chopped
1   medium onion, chopped fine
4   cloves fresh garlic, minced
½   teaspoon black pepper
½   cup dry sherry
1   lb. linguine
1   teaspoon salt
    Freshly grated Parmesan cheese and parsley sprigs for garnish.

Combine bouillon cube and water and boil for a few seconds, mixing thoroughly. Set aside. Heat oil in large, deep pot and saute mushrooms, prosciutto, onion, and garlic until onions and garlic are light golden brown. Add pepper, bouillon and sherry. Bring to boil, reduce heat and simmer for 10 minutes. Meanwhile, cook pasta in salted water until just done (*al dente*). Drain pasta and combine with sauce. Serve hot with Parmesan cheese, garnished with small parsley springs. Makes 6 servings.

ITALIAN MEATBALLS AND SAUCE FOR SPAGHETTI

This recipe is intended to serve 10 or more hungry people. You'll need a very large cooking pot (or use two smaller Dutch ovens) and be sure to watch it while cooking to prevent scorching.

Recipe contest entry: Teresa Traversone, Tucson, AZ

Meatballs
- 2 lb. lean ground beef
- 4 eggs, slightly beaten
- 1½ cups grated Parmesan and Romano cheese combined
- 1½ cups dry bread crumbs
- 1 cup milk
- 2 tablespoons chopped parsley
- 2 teaspoons salt
- ½ teaspoon garlic powder

Mix first 8 ingredients and shape into meatballs. Spray flat baking dish or pan with Pam and place meatballs in pan. Bake at 350 degrees for 30 minutes or until lightly browned. Meanwhile prepare sauce.

Sauce
- 1 onion, chopped
- ½ cup olive oil
- 2 teaspoons instant minced garlic
- 3 cans (12 oz. each) tomato paste
- 3 cans (15 oz. each) tomato sauce
- 3 cans (29 oz. each) whole tomatoes, chopped
- 2 teaspoons *each* oregano, garlic salt and Italian seasoning

In large heavy pot, brown onion in oil. Add minced garlic. Cook 1 minute longer. Add remaining ingredients including meatballs and simmer very gently for about 3 hours or until sauce is proper thickness. Serve over cooked spaghetti. Sprinkle with additional grated Italian cheese, if desired. Makes sauce for 10 or more servings.

GREEN RAVIOLI WITH GARLIC FILLING

What could be more appealing than homemade ravioli. Serve these with an "Alfredo" (cream) sauce, or make a sauce of melted butter, chopped parsley and minced garlic.

Recipe contest entry: James F. Benson, San Carlos, CA

Filling
- 12 oz. Monterey Jack cheese
- 3 cloves fresh garlic
- 12 oz. grated Parmesan cheese
- 12 oz. dry bread crumbs
  Fresh ground pepper
- 1 cup dry white wine
- 3 eggs

Process Jack cheese through food processor with grating blade. Remove cheese to bowl. With steel blade, process garlic. Add remaining dry ingredients and return Jack cheese to food processor container. Pulse until well mixed. Add wine to moisten, then eggs and pulse until mixed.

Ravioli Pasta
- 1 pkg. (10 oz.) frozen chopped spinach
- 2 cups unbleached white flour
- 1 tablespoon salt
- 1 tablespoon olive oil
- 2 eggs
  Water as needed

Cook spinach according to package directions. Drain, When cool, press water out of spinach. Chop with steel blade until finely chopped. Add flour and salt and mix. Add oil and mix. Add eggs and mix. Add water until a ball of dough is formed. Place on floured board. Knead until smooth and velvety. Place mixture in plastic bag for 1 hour. At this point, if you have a pasta machine, proceed to make dough. If not, roll only as much dough as you can handle at one time out on floured board until thin. On half the dough spread some of the filling and cover with other half of dough. With ravioli rolling pin or 1/8-inch board form ravioli, pressing rows of squares. Cut rows with pastry cutter or knife. In large pot of boiling water, cook ravioli until just done *al dente*. Drain and serve with sauce of your choice. Makes about 220 ravioli.

BAKED MANICOTTI WITH MEAT SAUCE

An excellent pasta dish, this recipe makes enough filling to stuff 14 manicotti with some left over.

Recipe contest entry: Vicki Hilton, Santa Barbara, CA

Sauce

      1   lb. lean ground beef
      1   lb. hot Italian sausage, casings removed
    ½   cup Italian bread crumbs
    ½   cup virgin olive oil
      3   cups chopped onion
      8   to 10 cloves fresh garlic, chopped
   2½ cups water
      2   cans (1 lb. 12 oz. each) Italian tomatoes, undrained
      9   oz. tomato paste
      4   tablespoons chopped parsley
      2   teaspoons *each* dried basil leaves and dried oregano leaves
   1½ tablesoons *each* sugar and salt
    ½   teaspoon pepper

Filling

      2   lb. ricotta cheese
      8   oz. Mozzarella cheese, chopped
    ⅓   cup grated Parmesan cheese
      1   tablespoon chopped parsley
      2   eggs
      1   teaspoon salt
    ½   teaspoon Italian seasoning
    ¼   teaspoon pepper
         Freshly grated Parmesan cheese for garnish

Place beef and sausage in skillet and brown thoroughly. Drain off grease; add bread crumbs and blend with meat. Set aside. In hot oil in 8 quart pot, saute onion and garlic 3 to 5 minutes. Mix in rest of sauce ingredients. Chop tomatoes into smaller pieces as they cook. Bring to boil, reduce heat and add meat mixture to sauce. Simmer, covered, stirring occasionally 1½ hours. Cook manicotti according to package directions; *parboil only.* Drain and set aside. Meanwhile combine all ingredients for filling and mix well with wooden spoon. After manicotti has cooled and dried, stuff them with spoon, being careful not to split them open. Set aside. In large casserole dish (8 to 10 quart) spread a thick layer of sauce. Neatly place stuffed manicotti close together on top of sauce. Add remainder of sauce until casserole is nearly full. Sprinkle with about ¼ cup Parmesan cheese. Bake, covered, at 350 degrees for 45 minutes or until bubbly; uncover and continue baking for another 10 to 15 minutes. Makes 10 to 12 servings.

MANTI

An easy-to-fix casserole with surprising flavor and rich sauce.

Recipe contest entry: Cindy Mayron, Gilroy, CA

1 pkg. (12 oz.) large shell pasta
¾ lb. ground lamb
1 tablespoon oil or butter
1 or 2 bunches green onions, minced
¼ cup chopped fresh parsley
4 cloves fresh garlic, minced
4 tablespoons butter
1 can (10¾ oz.) beef broth
1 can (8 oz.) tomato sauce

Cook pasta according to package directions. Drain and cool. Saute lamb lightly in oil or butter; combine with onions, parsley, and garlic; mix well. Stuff shells with meat mixture. Butter bottom of 3 quart baking dish with cover. Place shells in baking dish and dot with butter. Cover and bake in 350-degree oven for 20 minutes. Combine broth and tomato sauce in small pan and bring to boil. Pour over manti and bake 15 to 20 minutes longer until lamb is cooked and sauce thickens slightly. Makes 4 to 6 servings.

GLORIOSO FOR ONE PERSON

Although this recipe serves but one, it can be doubled, tripled or increased to fit any number you wish.

Recipe courtesy of: Jon Seeger

5 oz. shell pasta
2 tablespoons *each* butter and olive oil
¼ teaspoon crushed red pepper flakes
Salt and pepper
1½ large mushrooms, sliced
1 heaping tablespoon minced garlic
1 tablespoon minced parsley
½ cup grated Romano cheese

Cook pasta according to package directions. Meanwhile, heat butter and oil in saute pan until very hot, but do not brown. Add red pepper, pinch of salt and pepper and mushrooms and toss thoroughly. Add garlic, being careful not to burn garlic, reduce heat. When pasta is done, raise heat and add drained pasta to saute pan. Toss, add cheese and parsley and toss again. Makes 1 "glorioso" serving.

GARLIC-CHEESE MOSTACCIOLI

Great dish for a potluck originated by a finalist in the 1982 Recipe Contest who recommends serving it with his recipe for "Tomatoes a la William," also in this book.

Recipe contest entry: Bill Scales, Gilroy, CA

1   pkg. (12 oz.) mostaccioli
20 cloves fresh garlic, minced
1   large yellow onion, minced
4   tablespoons butter
    Freshly ground black pepper
1½ lb. Colby cheese, grated
½   cup dry white wine
¼   lb. Mozzarella cheese, grated
¼   cup chopped fresh parsley

Prepare mostaccioli according to package directions, using a little olive oil in water. Drain. Keep warm in shallow ovenproof baking dish. Saute garlic and onion in 2 tablespoons butter. Add pepper and set aside. Melt remaining 2 tablespoons butter in top of double boiler, add grated Colby cheese and stir in wine. When cheese has melted, combine with garlic-onion mixture and pour over mostaccioli. Sprinkle grated Mozzarella and parsley over; place on middle shelf of oven and broil for 1 to 2 minutes. Makes 10 servings.

SPINACH FETTUCCINE WITH ARTICHOKE SAUCE

A great pasta dish to serve with Thirty Clove Chicken (see page 134).

Recipe contest entry: Karen Harmatiuk, San Francisco, CA

2   jars (6 oz. each) marinated artichoke hearts, drained, reserving marinade
3   tablespoons butter
1   cup sliced mushrooms
¾   cup chopped walnuts
4   cloves fresh garlic, minced
3   tablespoons minced fresh basil *or* 1 tablespoon dried
1   cup ricotta cheese
¾   cup Parmesan cheese
½   cup heavy cream
1   pkg. (10 oz.) spinach fettuccine or equivalent homemade pasta

Coarsely chop artichoke hearts. Melt butter with reserved marinade in skillet. Saute artichokes, mushrooms, walnuts, garlic and basil just until tender. In blender, puree cheeses and cream. Mix well with artichoke mixture. Cook fettuccine according to package directions until *al dente*. Pour sauce over, toss to mix well and serve at once. Makes 6 servings.

PASTA TERESA

This tasty combination of artichoke hearts, tomatoes, garlic and thin spaghetti makes a great meal-in-a-hurry.

Recipe contest entry: Geoff Berkin, Los Angeles, CA

1 whole head garlic, peeled
3 tablespoons *each* chopped fresh basil and oregano
4 medium tomatoes
¾ cup olive oil
2 thick slices of onion
2 pkg. (9 oz. each) frozen artichoke hearts, thawed and drained
¾ lb. spaghettini
4 oz. grated Parmesan cheese
Salt and pepper to taste

In blender or food processor, puree garlic, basil and oregano. Slice each tomato into 8 or 10 thin wedges, then slice wedges in half. Heat oil in large skillet, add garlic puree and onion slices and saute over medium heat for about 2 to 3 minutes. Remove onion and discard. Add tomatoes and artichoke hearts to pan and gently mix. Lower heat and stir occasionally while pasta cooks. Cook pasta according to package directions until *al dente*. Drain. With slotted spoon, remove tomatoes and artichoke hearts from skillet to bowl. Add drained pasta to skillet and toss to coat with oil. Add Parmesan cheese and toss, then salt and pepper. Divide pasta onto four plates, then top with equal portions of tomatoes and artichoke hearts. Makes 4 servings.

TWO PEAS-IN-A-PASTA

A very tasty combination. Try it also with small egg noodles or macaroni.

Recipe contest entry: Mrs. J. Rhodes, Prescott, AZ

5 cloves fresh garlic, minced
6 tablespoons olive oil
1 pkg. (10 oz.) frozen peas
1 can (16 oz.) chick peas (garbanzos), drained, reserving liquid
1 teaspoon *each* dried basil and salt
1 lb. fettuccine or linguine
½ cup half-and-half
½ cup grated Parmesan cheese
¼ lb. Mozzarella cheese, grated

In 10-inch skillet, cook garlic in olive oil until golden but not brown. Add frozen peas and chick peas, basil and salt. Lower heat; cover and simmer for 10 minutes. Meanwhile, cook pasta according to package directions. Drain. In large serving dish, gently mix cooked pasta with half-and-half, Parmesan and Mozzarella. Pour cooked mixture over all, gently mixing through. Add reserved liquid if more moist pasta is desired. Makes 4 to 6 servings.

PASTA VERDE (SPAGHETTI WITH SPINACH AND ALMOND SAUCE)

Serve this pasta as a side dish with grilled or barbecued meats.

Recipe contest entry: Carole L. Rutter, Hayward, CA

1 bunch spinach *or* 1 pkg. (10 oz.) frozen spinach
¼ cup coarsely chopped fresh parsley
¼ cup *each* grated Romano and Parmesan cheese
¼ cup vegetable oil
2 tablespoons butter or margarine
1 oz. blanched almonds
4 or more cloves fresh garlic
¼ cup boiling water, plus extra on hand
1 lb. spaghetti or macaroni Parmesan cheese and chopped parsley for garnish

Wash spinach, remove white stems and chop leaves coarsely. Cook in small quantity of boiling salted water until tender *or* cook frozen spinach according to package directions. Drain, then place in blender with all remaining ingredients except hot water. Blend to smooth paste. Add boiling water, blend again for a few seconds. Extra water may be added to achieve desired consistency. Cook spaghetti according to package directions. Drain and pour sauce over; toss well. Garnish with extra Parmesan cheese and/or parsley if desired. Makes 4 to 6 servings.

NOTE: Sauce is best when served immediately, so time the cooking of the spaghetti to be ready when sauce is finished.

PATCHWORK CALICO PASTA

An excellent pasta dish which combines zucchini, broccoli, tomatoes and toasted pine nuts for unusual flavor and texture.

Recipe contest entry: Cynthia Kannenberg, Brown Deer, WI

4 zucchini, about ¾ lb., cut into diagonal slices
2 cups broccoli flowerets
½ cup pine nuts
3 fresh tomatoes
1 lb. spaghetti
¼ cup olive oil
1 tablespoon minced garlic
1 chile pepper (optional) Salt and pepper to taste
½ cup half-and-half or heavy cream
¼ cup butter
½ cup grated fresh Parmesan cheese

Blanch zucchini in boiling water for 1 minute, remove. Blanch broccoli for 3 to 4 minutes in boiling water. Drain. Peel and chop tomatoes. Toast pine nuts in 350-degree oven for 5 to 10 minutes being certain not to burn. Cook spaghetti as package directs until *al dente*. Drain. Heat oil in skillet; add garlic, zucchini, broccoli, tomatoes, chile peppers, and salt and pepper. Cook, briefly, stirring. Add drained spaghetti, cream, butter, cheese and nuts. Discard chile pepper. Toss and serve immediately. Garnish with additional cheese if desired. Makes 6 to 8 servings.

FUSILLI CON AGLIO, OLIO, PEPERONCINO E ZUCCHINI

This spicy pasta dish is also good chilled and served as a pasta salad.

Recipe contest entry: Laurie P. Farber, Sacramento, CA

1 zucchini, ends trimmed and coarsely chopped
⅔ cup olive oil
4 cloves fresh garlic
1 fresh jalapeno pepper, stem and seeds removed
1 tablespoon *each* fresh basil, thyme and oregano *or* 1 teaspoon dried
Dash *each* black and cayenne pepper, salt
1 can (16 oz.) cannellini beans, drained and rinsed
1 lb. fusilli (curly noodles)
Grated Parmesan, Romano, asiago or pecorino cheese (optional)
Garlic powder (optional)

In food processor or blender, combine zucchini, oil, garlic, jalapeno pepper, basil, thyme, oregano, black and red peppers and salt. Process with on-off motion until chopped but *not* pureed. Pour into small saucepan and simmer over low heat for about 5 minutes, stirring occasionally. Add drained and rinsed beans; simmer another 5 minutes until beans lose a bit of moisture. Meanwhile cook pasta according to package directions. Drain and pour sauce over, topping with grated cheese and a sprinkling of garlic powder, if desired. Makes 4 servings.

. . . under the pot lids of exciting ethnic cuisines garlic has sneaked back into town. The uppity little bulb is ever emerging as the prime seasoning in favored recipes. Suddenly it's chic to reek.

Town and Country

SAUSAGE AND RICE, SWISS STYLE

An excellent "quickie" meal. The caraway seed, frequently used in European cooking, adds a distinctive flavor to the dish. To serve 6, use 1½ lb. sausage, 1 cup rice and 2 cups stock.

Recipe contest entry: Christine Ammer, Lexington, MA

2 tablespoons margarine or vegetable oil
1 cup chopped onion
3 or more cloves fresh garlic, minced
1 lb. Polish sausage (Kielbasa), cut in 1-inch pieces
1½ cups chicken stock or broth
¾ cup rice
1 teaspoon caraway seed
Salt and pepper to taste

In large skillet, heat margarine and cook onion and garlic until onion is soft. Add sausage and cook, stirring, for 2 minutes. Stir in remaining ingredients. Bring to a boil, reduce heat and cover. Simmer for about 30 minutes or until rice is done and liquid has been absorbed. Makes 4 servings.

HOLLISTER HOT RICE

This recipe is a family favorite which is often prepared in double quantities since it is so popular.

Recipe contest entry: Christy Funk, Hollister, CA

2 cups long grain rice
6 or more cloves fresh garlic, minced
½ cup butter
2 cans (7 oz. each) whole green chiles
¼ lb. Jack or Cheddar cheese
2 cans (10½ oz. each) beef consomme (gelatin added) plus 2 consomme cans hot water

Saute rice and garlic in butter in skillet over medium heat for about 3 minutes. Divide rice mixture in half, spreading half on bottom of 13 x 9 x 2-inch baking dish. Wash chiles in cool water. Cut cheese in strips and insert into whole chiles. Lay stuffed chiles on rice mixture and spread remaining rice over. In a bowl mix soup and hot water thoroughly; then pour over rice and chiles. Cover tightly with foil to keep rice from drying out. Bake at 375 degrees for 40 to 50 minutes. Makes 8 servings.

CALIFORNIA PILAF

Although this recipe calls for the use of a "Crock-Pot," it can be made by using a Dutch oven or casserole and baking at 350-degrees for about 1 hour or until rice is tender and all liquid has been absorbed.

Recipe contest entry: E. Saavedra, Denver, CO

2 lb. ground beef
2½ cups water
2 cans (8 oz. each) tomato sauce
1⅓ cups long grain rice
⅔ cup sliced ripe olives
1 green bell pepper, seeded and chopped
1 small onion, chopped
3 cloves fresh garlic, minced
2½ teaspoons salt
¼ teaspoon pepper

Brown beef in skillet; drain off fat. Place beef and all remaining ingredients in 4 quart "Crock-Pot." Stir well. Cover and cook on low for 5 to 6 hours or on high for 3 hours. Makes 6 servings.

GARLIC DILL RICE

Garlic and herbs flavor this rice dish, an excellent accompaniment for roasted or broiled meats.

Recipe contest entry: Charles Valdes, Sacramento, CA

3 to 4 cloves fresh garlic, minced
2 tablespoons olive oil
1 cup rice
1 can (14½ oz.) chicken broth
1 teaspoon *each* dried dill and cilantro (coriander)
1 teaspoon salt
½ teaspoon onion powder

Saute garlic in hot oil until golden. Add rice and saute for 4 to 5 minutes over high heat. Add broth and seasonings. Bring back to boil, cover and simmer over low heat for 30 minutes. Fluff and mix rice and allow to stand uncovered for 5 minutes. Makes 4 to 6 servings.

Robust bulb reputed to give strength, courage.

Colorado Springs Gazette-Telegraph

MAHONY'S RICE

This colorful rice dish is the inspiration of the creator of Mahony's Bruschetta which won the 1983 Recipe Contest. Neil suggests serving it with barbecued meats "and a good Gewurztraminer." He also advises that it can be made in the morning, refrigerated and reheated just before serving.

Recipe contest entry: Neil Mahony, Ventura, CA

5 strips lean bacon, diced
1 medium onion, diced
1 medium green bell pepper, diced
8 cloves fresh garlic, chopped
1 cup long grain white rice, rinsed in cold water
⅓ cup plus 2 tablespoons soy sauce
1⅔ cups water
1 can (8 oz.) button mushrooms, drained
⅓ lb. cooked cocktail shrimp, fresh not canned
1 jar (4 oz.) diced pimentos, drained
6 tablespoons finely chopped fresh parsley

Fry bacon until crisp. Drain *thoroughly* and set aside. Fry onion, pepper and garlic in bacon grease until onions are translucent. Drain *thoroughly* and add to bacon. In saucepan combine rice with soy sauce and water and bring to a boil. Cover tightly, reduce heat and simmer for about 20 minutes or until all liquid is absorbed. Remove lid and leave pan on very low heat to drive off any remaining moisture. After about 10 minutes, stir in bacon mixture, add half the parsley and almost all of the mushrooms, shrimp and pimentos, saving some of each for garnish. Mix and transfer to shallow serving dish and garnish as desired. Serve at once. Makes 6 to 8 servings.

Meats

Regional Winner 1981 Recipe Contest   HELEN MIZE, Lakeland, FL

Lamb and garlic go together in a "garlicious" dish of rolled, stuffed lamb cutlets, topped with Olive Sauce and served over broad noodles. "Mighty good eating," says Ms. Mize.

GARLICIOUS LAMB ROLL-UPS

1½ pounds lamb cutlets
1½ teaspoons garlic salt
¼   teaspoon black pepper
2   slices bacon
2   tablespoons chopped onion
1   cup soft bread crumbs
1   tablespoon chopped parsley
1½ teaspoons dried mint leaves, crumbled
1   teaspoon lemon juice
1   large clove fresh garlic
¼   teaspoon crushed rosemary
¼   cup flour
3   tablespoons butter
    Olive Sauce (Recipe below)
1   (8 or 9 oz.) pkg. broad noodles

Pound lamb cutlets to flatten (or have butcher do this for you). Trim off edges to make 8 rectangles, about 5 x 7 inches. Sprinkle with garlic salt and pepper. Finely dice lamb trimmings (½ to 1 cup) and bacon. Brown lightly in skillet. Add onion and cook until tender. Stir in bread crumbs, parsley, mint, lemon juice, fresh garlic and rosemary. Spread stuffing on cutlets. Roll up, fasten with toothpicks and dredge in flour. Slowly brown on all sides in 3 tablespoons butter over moderately-low heat. Continue cooking until meat is tender, about 30 to 40 minutes. Meanwhile, prepare Olive Sauce, and cook noodles in boiling salted water as package directs, then drain well. Serve lamb rolls over noodles with sauce and crusty chunks of garlic bread. Makes 4 servings.

Olive Sauce
2   beef bouillon cubes
1½ cups hot water
2   tablespoons butter
2   tablespoons flour
1   tablespoon tomato paste
1   bay leaf
⅓   cup sliced stuffed green olives
2   tablespoons dry sherry
    Garlic salt and pepper to taste

Dissolve 2 beef bouillon cubes in 1½ cups hot water. In a medium-sized saucepan melt 2 tablespoons butter and blend in 2 tablespoons flour. Slowly stir in broth. Cook, stirring until thickened. Add remaining ingredients, stir and season to taste.

Third Prize Winner 1982 Recipe Contest   JOHN ROBINSON, Granada Hills, CA

This hearty award-winning entree which won a third prize for its originator requires 30 cloves of fresh garlic to achieve its robust flavor. If you'd like even more garlic flavor, stud the lamb with slivers of fresh garlic before cooking.

LAMB SHANKS WITH BARLEY AND GARLIC

Lamb

4   lamb shanks
¼   cup *each* butter and olive oil
½   cup *each* red table wine and water
½   teaspoon rosemary (more if desired)
30   cloves fresh garlic, peeled

In ovenproof pan with tight fitting lid, brown lamb on all sides in butter and olive oil. Remove lamb, stir wine and water into pan and heat, scraping bottom and sides of pan. Replace lamb and sprinkle with rosemary. Add at least 30 cloves garlic. Put a sheet of foil over top, then the tight fitting lid to seal thoroughly. Bake at 350 degrees for 1½ hours. Prepare barley.

Barley

½   to ¾ lb. fresh mushrooms, sliced
½   cup butter
1½   cups pearl barley
2½   to 3½ cups beef bouillon
2   tablespoons mint jelly

Saute mushrooms in ¼ cup butter and set aside. Brown barley in remaining ¼ cup butter until golden brown. Mix in mushrooms, turn into casserole, and add 2½ cups beef bouillon. Cover and bake 30 minutes at 350 degrees. Add more bouillon as needed, about 1 cup, and cook, uncovered, until liquid is absorbed and barley is done.

To serve, arrange lamb shanks around edges of serving platter. Add garlic cloves to barley, and heap in center of platter. Stir mint jelly into liquid remaining, cook 3 to 5 minutes, and spoon over lamb. Makes 4 servings.

Regional Winner 1982 Recipe Contest   CHAD REOTT, West Hollywood, CA

More than a seasoning, garlic is a major ingredient in this excellent dish. Chad recommends pouring a hefty glass of wine before starting to separate and peel the 30 heads of garlic. It will help to cheer you through the task.

CHAD'S GARLIC LAMB

6- to 7-lb. leg of lamb
30 *heads* of fresh garlic, cloves separated and peeled
1 large onion, peeled
Garlic powder
Onion powder
Italian seasoning
½ gal. dry red wine such as Burgundy
3 tablespoons cornstarch

Coarsely chop 10 to 12 cloves garlic and onion; set aside. Spread remaining whole garlic cloves over bottom of roasting pan. With metal skewer poke holes in lamb (lengthwise). Stuff holes with chopped garlic and onion (a chopstick simplifies this step). Sprinkle lamb generously with garlic and onion powder and seasoning. Nestle lamb generously with garlic and onion powder and seasoning. Nestle lamb into bed of garlic cloves and pour enough wine over to reach a depth of ¾ inch. Roast lamb uncovered in 325-degree oven for about 30 minutes per lb. or until lamb is done to your liking. Remove lamb to warm platter. Pour contents of pan into blender and liquify. Transfer to sauce pan. Mix 1 cup wine with cornstarch and add to liquid; heat until sauce is thickened. Carve lamb and pour some sauce over. Pass remaining sauce. Makes 6 servings.

Eat leeks in tide and garlic in May, and all the year after physicians may play.

Russian proverb

Regional Winner 1982 Recipe Contest

ROWENA BERGMAN, Toronto, Ontario, Canada

Plan ahead if you want to try this lamb dish. It is best if marinated for about 4 days in the refrigerator. For extra browning, run it under broiler for a few minutes just before serving.

RACK OF LAMB BREADBIN

1	rack of lamb, about 5 to 6 pounds
¾	cup cloves fresh garlic, peeled
½	cup olive oil
	Juice of 4 lemons
3	heaping tablespoons dry mustard
2	heaping tablespoons bouquet garni
1	heaping tablespoon tarragon

Have the butcher cut through chine bone so meat can be carved into individual chops at the table and trim off fat around ends of ribs and around kidney area. Combine garlic and all remaining ingredients in food processor bowl (or in blender) and process until liquified. Place roast in large plastic bag, add marinade, spreading it all over roast and between cuts made by butcher. Seal bag and refrigerate at least 2 days. To roast, remove from bag, place in roasting pan and insert meat thermometer in thickest part of meat. Roast at 450 degrees until thermometer registers "medium" for beef. The lamb will be medium rare at this point. If you wish to have it done more, follow thermometer accordingly. Makes 4 servings.

Finalist in 1983 Recipe Contest: RAYMOND G. MARSHALL, Pasadena, CA

Some of the ingredients in this recipe may sound a bit exotic, but you'll like the results. The pork and chicken are marinated in advance to give the meat a rich flavor. Canned, peeled lichees are available in most supermarkets or you can substitute chunks of drained canned pineapple, but it won't taste the same!

PORK AND CHICKEN LOS ARCOS

3 lb. pork shoulder
2 lb. chicken thighs
40 cloves fresh garlic, unpeeled
1 tablespoon salt
1 cup vinegar
2 tablespoons lemon juice
8 bay leaves
½ teaspoon *each* fresh ground pepper and caramel coloring
4 whole cloves
6 very thin slices fresh ginger (or prepared in light syrup)
2 tablespoon salad oil
2 tablespoons plain gelatin
2 cans (11 oz. each) peeled lichees
1 cup toasted pumpkin seeds

Cut pork into 1½ inch cubes. Bone chicken and cut each thigh into 3 or 4 pieces. Prepare marinade: Peel, chop and mash 4 cloves garlic in salt to make a paste. Add vinegar, lemon juice, bay leaves, pepper, caramel coloring, cloves and ginger; mix well. Pour over pork and chicken and marinate for 6 to 8 hours in the refrigerator, stirring frequently. Remove pork and chicken from marinade and reserve marinade. Saute pork in oil for 20 minutes. Add chicken and saute for another 20 minutes. Then add the remaining 36 cloves unpeeled garlic. Add gelatin to reserved marinade to soften, adding a little water if necessary. Stir marinade well, add to pork and chicken and cook about 30 minutes or until meat is done and tender. Add drained lichees and seeds to pot. Let cook about 5 minutes to heat through and serve, preferably with steamed rice. Makes 8 servings.

Note: The garlic cloves are eaten using the fingers to pinch the clove out of its skin.

Finalist in 1982 Recipe Contest:　　　SANDY HOILES, Sunnyvale, CA

This recipe was named by the happy group who first sampled it and exclaimed "Ole!" Don't worry about small chunks of tamale which might fall out of the steak rolls; they add an interesting texture to the sauce.

FLANK STEAK OLE

1　flank steak, (2 to 2½ lb.) tenderized
10　cloves fresh garlic (about 1 head)
½　teaspoon salt
¼　teaspoon pepper
1　teaspoon chili powder
1　can (15 oz.) tamales, papers discarded and sauce reserved
¼　cup flour
2　to 3 tablespoons olive oil
1　can (8 oz.) tomato sauce
1　cup red table wine
⅓　cup grated Parmesan cheese

Stretch steak gently without tearing to a rectangular shape. Press 3 cloves garlic over meat, sprinkle with salt, pepper and chili powder. Crumble tamales over steak, spreading to within 1 inch of edges. Roll up, making a firm roll but not too tight and tie with string at intervals or secure with skewers. Dust with flour, shaking off excess. Heat oil in Dutch oven or heavy pan with cover and brown roll on all sides over medium-high heat. Reduce heat to low. Pour tomato sauce over roll. Measure wine into tomato sauce can and pour into tamale can with its reserved sauce. Press remaining 7 cloves garlic into this sauce, stir, and pour *around* roll not over it. Cover and simmer until tender, about 2 to 2½ hours. Remove from heat and remove string or skewers, disturbing topping as little as possible. Sprinkle with cheese and return to low heat. Cover and cook until cheese melts, about 20 minutes. Place roll on serving platter and cut into 1-inch slices. Pass sauce separately in gravy boat or bowl. (Chunks of tamale that fall our of the roll add interesting texture to the sauce.) Makes 4 servings.

Regional Winner 1983 Recipe Contest   DAVID LINDLEY, Union City, GA

Cooking for one? Pamper yourself with this delicious, garlic-laced veal chop with peppers.

VEAL GARLIC CHOP

1 veal chop, approximately 14 oz.
1 tablespoon crushed black peppercorns
   Salt to taste
2 tablespoons butter
1 tablespoon olive oil
1 green bell pepper
1 red bell pepper
1 medium onion, peeled
6 cloves fresh garlic, minced
1 teaspoon finely chopped fresh parsley

Rub veal chop all over with crushed black peppercorns and salt to taste. In heavy skillet, combine butter and oil until hot, but not smoking; add veal and reduce heat to medium. Brown veal for about 7 minutes, then turn and brown other side. Meanwhile, remove seeds and membrane from peppers. Slice peppers and onion into julienne strips and add to skillet with veal. Add pinch of salt. Spread garlic evenly over chop; cover skillet and cook about 10 minutes, stirring vegetables occasionally until tender. To serve, arrange bell peppers and onion on plate, top with veal chop and sprinkle with parsley. Serves 1 generously.

How anything as small and delicate looking as a clove of garlic can have such an impact on food never ceases to amaze.

Betsy Balsley
Los Angeles Times

Finalist in 1983 Recipe Contest: JOHN ROBINSON, Granada Hills, CA

This two-time finalist specializes in hearty dishes made with grains and legumes. In this casserole, rabbit is paired with lentils and finished with the fruity sweetness of apple. An attractive and satisfying meal.

RABBIT WITH LENTILS

   8 rabbit legs and thighs
      Flour, as needed
   ½ cup butter, unsalted
   ¼ cup olive oil
   1 lb. dried lentils
      Salt and pepper to taste
      Cayenne
   ½ lb. thick-sliced bacon, cut
      into 2-inch pieces
  20 to 25 cloves fresh garlic,
      peeled
  1½ cups thickly sliced fresh
      mushrooms
   ½ cup gin (with strong
      juniper berry flavor)
   ½ cup crabapple jelly
   ½ cup finely chopped
      parsely
   1 can (or jar) red spiced
      crabapples
   1 bunch watercress

Dredge rabbit in flour and saute over moderately high heat in ¼ cup *each* butter and olive oil until brown on all sides. Remove rabbit and save pan with drippings. Cook lentils according to package instructions, except stop when *slightly* underdone. Drain lentils, stir in remaining ¼ cup butter, and season with salt, pepper and a generous dash cayenne. Line bottom of heavy casserole (with tightly fitting lid) with bacon. Put layer of lentils on top of bacon, add rabbit pieces, heap garlic around rabbit and cover all with balance of lentils. Spread mushrooms on top and seal casserole with aluminum foil. Then carefully put on the lid and bake at 350 degrees for 1½ hours. Remove rabbit from casserole and place around edge of serving platter. Stir balance of casserole ingredients together and mount in center of platter. Heat pan with reserved drippings over moderately high heat, add gin and stir until thoroughly deglazed. Add crabapple jelly and stir until completely combined. Remove from heat, add parsley and stir. Pour over rabbit. Garnish with crabapples and watercress. Serves 4.

JOHN'S NEAPOLITAN BEEF ENTREE

An everyday casserole that bakes with a crusty cheese topping and plenty of good garlic flavor.

Recipe contest entry: Vicki Leffler, Independence, KY

⅓ cup chopped onion
4 or more cloves fresh garlic, crushed
1 cup diced carrots
½ cup diced celery
¼ cup salad oil
1½ lb. ground chuck
1 can (16 oz.) tomatoes
1 can (6 oz.) mushrooms, drained
1 can (6 oz.) tomato paste
½ cup sherry
1 teaspoon salt
½ teaspoon *each* pepper, dried oregano and basil

8 oz. shell macaroni, cooked
1 pkg. (9 or 10 oz.) frozen spinach, drained
1 cup grated sharp Cheddar cheese
½ cup buttered bread crumbs
Parmesan cheese

Saute onion, garlic, carrots and celery in oil for 5 minutes. Add meat; cook and stir until lightly browned. Add next 8 ingredients. Simmer, uncovered, for 1½ hours. Add macaroni and spinach; mix well. Turn into 2-quart casserole. Top with Cheddar cheese and bread crumbs. Bake uncovered at 325 degrees for about 30 minutes or until hot. Serve with Parmesan cheese. Makes about 8 servings.

HERBED POT ROAST
WITH EGGPLANT AND TOMATOES

This pot roast marinates in a garlic-herb mixture for extra flavor for 8 hours before being baked in the oven. Eggplant is a surprise ingredient.

Recipe contest entry: Anonymous

4	to 5-lb. chuck or other well-marbled beef roast
12	cloves fresh garlic, finely chopped
1	cup plus 2 tablespoons olive oil
¼	cup red wine vinegar
2	tablespoons lemon juice
2	tablespoons dried basil
1	onion, chopped
1	medium eggplant, cubed
1	cup Italian plum tomatoes
2	tablespoons tomato paste

Marinate beef in Garlic Marinade made by combining 8 cloves finely chopped garlic, ¾ cup olive oil, wine vinegar, lemon juice and dried basil, for 8 hours, turning often. Remove from marinade and pat meat dry. Reserve marinade. Heat remaining 6 tablespoons oil in skillet; add onions and remaining 4 cloves finely chopped garlic and cook until transparent. Add beef and brown on all sides. Transfer meat and onion-garlic mixture to large Dutch oven. Add reserved marinade, eggplant and tomatoes. Cover and bake at 350 degrees for about 2 hours or until meat thermometer inserted into the center of the roast registers "rare." Remove meat to platter and keep hot. Skim fat from mixture in pot and spoon remaining juices over sliced beef. Makes 6 servings.

Now the pungent bulb is back in favor, its nervy aroma drifting from the best kitchens to enhance many a little dinner party.

Town and Country

ROAST WITH GARLIC / DILL SAUCE

Dill pickle is one ingredient that gives this pot roast its piquante flavor. The addition of sour cream at the last minute helps to blend all the flavors into a delicious sauce.

Recipe contest entry: Alexis Ann Smith, Bowie, MD

4 lbs. boneless rolled beef rump roast
1 teaspoon *each* salt and white pepper
½ teaspoon ginger
2 tablespoons bacon grease
½ cup dry white wine
   Water
2 cups sliced mushrooms
4 cloves fresh garlic, minced
2 tablespoons *each* chopped dill pickle and chopped pimento
1 tablespoon chopped fresh parsley
¾ teaspoon caraway seed
2 tablespoons cornstarch
2 tablespoons dill pickle juice
¾ cup sour cream at room temperature

Sprinkle roast with salt, pepper and ginger. In Dutch oven, brown roast on all sides in hot grease. Add wine, cover and simmer for 2½ hours. Remove roast and keep warm. Skim fat from drippings, add enough water to make 1½ cups broth in pan. Add mushrooms, garlic, pickle, pimento, parsley, and caraway seed. Blend cornstarch with pickle juice and 2 tablespoons water. Add to pan. Cook, stirring, for 5 minutes. Gradually blend in the sour cream. Heat through. Slice meat and serve with sauce. Makes 6 to 8 servings.

Gilroy is an example of well-managed small-town living that could have remained a secret....., except for a festival it hosts annually called the Gilroy Garlic Festival.

Ford Times

POT ROAST A LA GILROY

Red wine and coffee help to create an abundance of rich brown gravy to serve with this pot roast over noodles, potatoes or rice.

Recipe contest entry: Sylvia Barber, Danville, CA

8   or more cloves fresh garlic
1   large onion
4- to 5-lb. lean chuck roast
1   cup dry red wine, prefer-
    ably Burgundy
3   tablespoons oil
2   cups strong black coffee
1   bay leaf
    Water
    Salt and pepper to taste
    (or part seasoned salt)
2   tablespoon cornstarch

Peel garlic and onion and slice into lengthwise strips. Pierce roast all the way through in several places with a sharp knife. Stuff 2 or 3 slivers of garlic and 1 or 2 slices of onion into each slit. Place in enamel, glass or stainless steel pan and pour wine over. Cover and refrigerate 24 to 48 hours, turning occasionally. Drain wine and reserve. Pat roast dry and brown in hot oil in large pot until very well browned. Drain off excess fat and discard. Add coffee, bay leaf and enough water mixed with the reserved red wine to make 2 cups. Bring to a boil, then simmer for 2 to 3 hours. Add salt and pepper during last half hour of cooking. Remove meat and bay leaf from pot. Mix cornstarch and water to make a thin paste. Add to simmering liquid and stir until thickened. Return meat to gravy or slice and pour gravy over. Serve with mashed potatoes, noodles or rice. Makes 6 to 8 servings.

The herb of mirth and medicine, remedy and rancor will be abundant in all its forms.

1001 Home Ideas Magazine

GARLIC SPARERIBS

Whether they are served as a main course or as an appetizer, these steamed ribs are outstanding. If you don't have a steamer, simply place ribs on a plate on a rack in large covered pot or wok.

Recipe contest entry: Erline Dair, South San Francisco, CA

3 lb. spareribs
8 cloves fresh garlic, finely chopped
6 tablespoons *each* soy sauce and oyster sauce
3 tablespoons dry sherry
   Hot chili oil (optional)
   Chopped green onions (optional)

Chop spareribs into bite-sized pieces. Cover with water and bring to a boil. Parboil spareribs for 10 minutes. Drain and rinse with cold water. Combine remaining ingredients except chili oil and green onion. Mix with spareribs and place on a heatproof dish on rack in steamer. Steam for 45 minutes. Garnish with green onions and serve with optional chili oil, if desired. Makes 4 servings.

TENTH ANNIVERSARY RIBS

This recipe was developed in honor of a tenth wedding anniversary. It combines the lightly sweet flavor Jill likes and the peppery spice Ron enjoys and "oh, that wonderful garlic!"

Recipe contest entry: Jill Goddard and Ron Kraus, Newhall, CA

8 cloves fresh garlic, minced
3 cans (8 oz. each) tomato sauce
3 small onions, minced
2 cups red wine
1 can (4 oz.) diced green chiles
5 tablespoons maple syrup
3 tablespoons *each* soy sauce and red wine vinegar
2 tablespoons prepared mustard
1 tablespoon Worcestershire sauce
1 teaspoon celery seed
½ teaspoon black pepper
¼ teaspoon *each* cayenne pepper and smoke salt
3 to 4 lb. beef or pork ribs.

Combine all ingredients except ribs in a large enamel kettle. Bring to boil, reduce heat and allow to simmer uncovered for 1 hour, stirring occasionally. Meanwhile, place ribs in a deep pot; cover with water. Bring to boil, cover and simmer for 45 minutes to 1 hour to remove fat and tenderize ribs. Remove ribs to shallow baking pan, pour sauce over and bake for 30 minutes, at 350 degrees, turning and basting occasionally. Makes 2 to 3 servings.

SPARERIBS A LA GILROY

Chinese Five Spice Powder, an essential ingredient in this easy-to-make recipe for spareribs, is available in Oriental markets or in the Oriental food section of most supermarkets.

Recipe contest entry: Lori Allen, Tacoma, WA

⅔ cup soy sauce
⅓ cup maple syrup
8 cloves fresh garlic, minced
3 tablespoons peach brandy
2 teaspoons *each* Five Spice Powder and ground ginger
2 lb. spareribs

In a bowl combine all ingredients except ribs and mix well. Place ribs in shallow dish, pour mixture over and turn ribs to coat. Marinate for 2 hours, covered, turning them about every 15 minutes. Place ribs in one layer on rack over shallow baking pan in 450-degree oven. Pour boiling water to 1 inch in bottom of pan. Brush ribs with marinade and bake for 30 minutes. Turn ribs, brush with more marinade. Reduce heat to 350 degrees and continue baking for 45 minutes, turning ribs once more. Transfer ribs to board and chop into 3-inch lengths. Makes 4 servings.

SUMPTUOUS SPARERIBS

Cooking time in this recipe may vary depending on how meaty the ribs are. Check every half hour and test for tenderness. When ribs are fork tender, they are ready to serve.

Recipe contest entry: Dorothy Jenkins, Livermore, CA

4 lb. pork spareribs, cut in serving-size pieces
10 cloves fresh garlic, peeled
1 onion, chopped fine
1 tablespoon margarine
1 cup *each* catsup and water
6 tablespoons brown sugar
¼ cup chopped celery *or* 1 tablespoon celery salt
4 tablespoons lemon juice
2 tablespoons *each* vinegar and Worcestershire sauce
1 tablespoon ground mustard
¼ teaspoon cayenne pepper

Place spareribs in baking pan with cover. Split 6 cloves garlic at the top to release flavor and sprinkle over ribs. Cover pan and bake at 350 degrees for 1 hour. Pour off the grease. Mince remaining 4 cloves garlic and fry with onions in margarine until onion is transparent, being careful not to burn garlic. Add all remaining ingredients and pour over ribs evenly. Cover and bake at 350 degrees, basting every ½ hour and checking with fork for doneness. May take up to 2 hours. Bake uncovered for the last ½ hour. Makes 4 servings.

ANGELA'S MILANESE

An inexpensive version of a classic recipe substituting thin sliced round steak for veal.

Recipe contest entry: Angela Vannucci, Fremont, CA

¾ lb. lean round steak, sliced thin (slice steak once through horizontally)
1 egg
¼ cup water
1 cup plain bread crumbs
¼ cup olive oil, approximately
5 to 6 cloves fresh garlic
Pinch of salt
2 dried hot chile peppers, finely chopped
Peel of ½ lemon, cut into thin strips
2 sprigs fresh rosemary without stems
2 cans (8 oz. each) tomato sauce

Dip steak in egg which has been beaten with water. Dredge meat in crumbs. Pour olive oil into large skillet to ⅛ inch and heat until very hot. Brown steak quickly in oil turning once, until golden, adding more oil if needed. Remove from skillet and drain on paper towel. Wipe out skillet and pour about ¹⁄₁₆ inch oil. Heat to very hot. Chop garlic with salt and add with chile peppers, lemon peel and rosemary to hot oil; saute briefly then add tomato sauce and meat. Gently cover meat with sauce and simmer over low heat for at least 30 minutes. Makes 3 to 4 servings.

BUFFET MEAT LOAF

This recipe bakes in two loaf pans, making enough meat loaf for about six people. If there's any left over, it slices very well when chilled.

Recipe contest entry: Terry Santana, Saratoga, CA

3 lb. lean ground chuck
½ lb. fresh spinach, washed and coarsely chopped
8 cloves fresh garlic, minced
2 cups soft bread crumbs
1 large onion, chopped
1 tablespoon Madeira wine
2 teaspoons dried thyme
1 tablespoon salt
1½ teaspoon pepper
1 teaspoon ground cumin
½ teaspoon crumbled rosemary
3 raw eggs
8 hard-cooked eggs, whole

In large mixing bowl, combine ground chuck, spinach, garlic, bread crumbs, onion, wine and seasonings. Beat raw eggs lightly and add. Lightly toss all ingredients together. Using two 6-cup loaf pans, layer ¼ of meat mixture into each pan. Lay a row of 4 eggs down center of each loaf. Top eggs with remaining meat, smoothing top. Place on baking sheet in 350 degree oven and bake for 1½ hours. Allow loaves to cool 10 minutes, then invert on platter and serve. Makes 6 to 8 servings.

QUICKIE CUBE STEAKS

Fast and easy and, best of all, "delicioso."

Recipe contest entry: Ann Laramee, Los Angeles, CA

4   cube steaks
4   slices American or
    Monterey Jack cheese
4   cloves fresh garlic,
    minced
1   can (4 oz.) diced green
    chiles
    Salt and pepper to taste
2   tablespoons oil or butter,
    or combination

On each cube steak, place 1 slice of cheese and top with garlic, chiles and salt and pepper. Roll up and fasten with toothpicks. In a skillet fry steaks in oil until meat is browned and cooked to your liking. Makes 4 servings.

VEAL FRICASSEE WITH GARLIC

A buffet dish that is definitely company fare, but why not treat the family, too?

Recipe contest entry: Susan Grossman, Tucson, AZ

1   lb. veal stew meat cut in ½
    inch cubes
6   tablespoon flour
    seasoned with salt and
    pepper
3   tablespoons butter
2   tablespoons cooking oil
1   cup coarsely minced
    onions
3   large cloves fresh garlic,
    minced or pressed
½   lb. fresh mushrooms,
    sliced thin
½   cup dry white wine
½   cup veal or chicken stock
    or water
½   cup heavy cream
1   tablespoon minced fresh
    parsley

Dredge veal in flour and shake off excess. Heat butter and oil in heavy skillet and brown veal in batches until golden. With slotted spoon, remove veal to platter and keep warm. Add onions, garlic and mushrooms to skillet, cover and cook until onions are soft. Remove all from skillet with slotted spoon and add to platter with veal. Pour off any remaining butter or oil from skillet and discard. Add wine and deglaze, scraping up all brown bits; cook for 2 minutes. Return veal and vegetables to skillet, add stock or water, cover and simmer for 30 minutes or until veal is tender and sauce is thickened. About 10 minutes before serving, add cream and simmer another 5 minutes until sauce is thick. Pour veal and sauce onto hot serving platter and sprinkle with minced parsley. Serve with broad egg noodles or rice. Makes 4 servings.

CHOW YUK

On Chinese restaurant menus this dish usually contains a wide variety of vegetables and this recipe is no exception. It also calls for "fresh Chinese noodles." If not available, substitute dried noodles or rice.

Recipe contest entry: Barbara Towe, Gilroy, CA

1½ lb. flank steak
½ cup soy sauce
6 cloves fresh garlic, peeled
3 tablespoons peanut oil
3 slices fresh ginger
½ lb. fresh mushrooms, sliced
¼ lb. fresh bean sprouts
¼ lb. fresh sugar peas, blanched (optional)
1 can (5 oz.) water chestnuts, drained and sliced
1 green bell pepper, seeded and cut into slivers
1 medium tomato, cut into eighths
   Fresh Chinese noodles, cooked and fried

Cut flank steak in half lengthwise; slice each half diagonally into thin slices. Marinate in ¼ cup soy sauce and 3 sliced garlic cloves for 2 to 3 hours. Heat oil in a wok or large skillet. Stir-fry ginger and 3 whole garlic cloves, discarding both when lightly browned. Stir-fry meat quickly until brown and add remaining ¼ cup soy sauce. Cover and steam meat for 45 seconds. Transfer meat to a platter and keep warm. To the liquid in the pan add all the vegetables except the tomato. Stir-fry for about 1 minute. Return meat to wok and mix thoroughly with the vegetables. Add tomato wedges on top, cover and cook for 1 minute. Serve meat and vegetables with remaining liquid on top of Chinese noodles. Makes 4 servings.

VEAL CUTLET PARMIGIANA

For the best flavor, be sure to use a good Italian Parmesan and grate it just before preparing the recipe.

Recipe contest entry: Carole A. Lake, Gilroy, CA

4 veal cutlets, pounded very thin
  Flour
4 large eggs, beaten
  Plain bread crumbs
¼ cup olive oil
½ cup butter
⅛ cup chopped chives
3 cloves fresh garlic, smashed and chopped fine
2½ cups marinara sauce (spicy tomato sauce)
4 slices prosciutto (thin sliced Italian ham)
4 slices Mozzarella cheese
  Salt and pepper to taste
  Grated Parmesan cheese

Dip cutlets into flour, then into egg and then bread crumbs. Repeat. Saute breaded cutlets for 6 minutes in oil and half of the butter. Melt remaining butter and add chives and garlic. Set aside and keep warm. Pour a layer of marinara sauce on the bottom of a baking dish. Place cutlets on top of sauce and pour a little sauce over. Cover each cutlet with a slice of prosciutto; then pour garlic, chives and butter over. Place a slice of cheese on top and lightly salt and pepper. Spoon remaining marinara sauce on top to cover meat. Sprinkle with grated cheese. Bake uncovered at 350 degrees for 20 minutes. Serve at once. Makes 4 servings.

Gilroy, California. Population 20,000. Except in early August. Then it swells fivefold. One hundred thousand people going bananas over GARLIC!

TWA Ambassador Magazine

LAMB SHANKS A LA BASQUE

This recipe was developed over 30 years ago and has been embellished and improved over the years to near perfection.

Recipe contest entry: M. Bernal, Morgan Hill, CA

4   meat lamb shanks
½   cup plus 2 tablespoons salad oil
10 cloves fresh garlic
½   lb. fresh mushrooms
½ to 1 cup chicken broth
½   cup dry red wine (Burgundy)
1   cup navy beans
Salt and pepper to taste
½   cup chopped fresh parsley
¼   cup wine vinegar

In heavy Dutch oven brown lamb shanks in 2 tablespoons salad oil. Remove lamb and reserve. Add 4 cloves garlic and mushrooms; brown well. Return lamb to Dutch oven and add wine and ½ cup broth. Cook, covered, in 350-degree oven for about 2 hours, adding more broth as needed, until meat falls from bones. Meanwhile cook beans with 4 cloves garlic in water to cover until soft. Drain and remove garlic. Remove bones from lamb. Add beans and salt and pepper to cooked meat and heat through. Serve with a sauce made by combining ½ cup salad oil, 2 minced cloves garlic, parsley and vinegar. Makes 4 servings.

Driving north from San Juan Bautista you can usually count on abundant advance warning that you are approaching Gilroy. When the wind is blowing the right . . . way, the unmistaken aroma of garlic can be detected in the air for many miles around.

Michael Dorman

GLORIA'S LAMB STEW

This is lamb stew with a difference—chile peppers, garlic and fresh cilantro are the seasonings.

Recipe contest entry: Gloria Park, Los Gatos, CA

1 cup fresh cilantro leaves (coriander)
1 whole head fresh garlic, peeled
2 or 3 fresh hot red or green peppers, seeded
½ cup olive oil
2 medium onions, finely chopped
4 lb. lean boneless lamb, cut into 1-inch cubes
Salt and freshly ground pepper to taste
⅔ cup fresh orange juice
⅓ cup lime or lemon juice
Water
2 lb. potatoes, peeled and sliced
1 lb. fresh green peas, helled *or* 2 pkg. frozen

In blender or food processor puree cilantro, garlic and peppers; set aside. Heat oil in casserole or Dutch oven and saute onions until soft. Stir in cilantro mixture and cook for a minute or two longer. Add lamb pieces and cook for about 5 minutes, turning to coat with sauce. Season to taste with salt and a generous amount of pepper. Add orange and lime or lemon juice and enough water to cover, about 1½ cups. Cover and simmer until lamb is tender, about 1½ hours. If desired, this dish may be refrigerated at this point in order to solidify and remove any excess fat. Let stand to bring to room temperature before heating. Boil potatoes and peas separately in salted water until tender. Drain and add to casserole. Bring casserole to a simmer and cook just long enough to heat through. Makes 4 to 5 servings.

Garlic: Eat it with someone you love.

Fayetteville Observer

MARINATED GRILLED LEG OF LAMB

Menu suggestions from the chef to serve with the lamb: Baked Potatoes with Butter and Feta Cheese, Tomatoes and Sugar Snap Peas Vinaigrette, Homemade Sourdough Rolls and Fresh Raspberries and Cream.

Recipe contest entry: Linda Nee, Keller, WA

7- to 9-lb. leg of lamb
10 cloves fresh garlic, finely chopped
 1 cup honey
 1 cup soy sauce
 ⅓ cup dry sherry

Bone and butterfly lamb or have butcher do it. In a small bowl, combine garlic, honey, soy sauce and sherry. Place lamb in large roasting pan or large shallow baking dish. Pour marinade over, cover with plastic wrap and let stand at room temperature for at least 12 hours or overnight. If desired, lamb can be marinated for 3 or 4 days in refrigerator, but be sure to allow to come to room temperature before grilling. Grill lamb over hot coals to desired state of doneness. (For rare, allow approximately 15 to 20 minutes per side.) Let meat rest for 5 to 10 minutes before carving. If desired, heat remaining marinade and serve as sauce for the meat.

The best thing to do with garlic of course, is to eat it.

Sylvia Rubin
San Francisco Chronicle

ORANGE-GARLIC PORK CHOPS

The flavors of garlic, onion and ginger combined with the tang of fresh orange help to transform these pork chops into a truly exotic main course.

Recipe contest entry: Grace Maduell and Reid Brennen, San Rafael, CA

6 pork chops
1 medium orange
4 cloves fresh garlic
½ small onion
¼ teaspoon powdered
   ginger
   Pepper
1 to 2 tablespoons butter
   Salt to taste

Remove fat from chops. Squeeze orange into small bowl, keeping as much pulp as possible. Press garlic into orange juice. Using garlic press, squeeze onion into orange-garlic mixture, being sure to remove onion skin. Add ginger and a pinch of pepper; stir well. Place chops in shallow baking dish, cover with marinade and let stand for at least 45 minutes. Melt butter in skillet with lid. Remove chops from marinade, reserving marinade, and brown chops on both sides in butter. Cover with remaining marinade and cook, covered, for 10 minutes. Remove cover and cook until fork tender. Add salt and pepper to taste. Makes 6 servings.

SPICY CHOPS AND CABBAGE

Apples and cabbage are favorite ingredients in German cuisine. Combined here with garlic in a sauce for thick pork chops they produce a deliciously different meal for the family.

Recipe contest entry: Margie Opresik, Phillips, WI

4   pork loin chops, ¾ inch thick
3   cloves fresh garlic, peeled
4   tablespoons water
1   teaspoon salt
½   small bay leaf
3   medium apples, peeled, cored and coarsely chopped
1   medium head cabbage, cored and coarsely chopped
½   small onion, chopped
¼   cup sugar
2   tablespoon *each* vinegar and water
1½ teaspoon flour

Trim fat from chops an cook fat in skillet to oil surface. Discard fat and brown chops in skillet. Add garlic, 2 tablespoons water, ½ teaspoon salt and bay leaf; cover and simmer for 30 minutes. Remove chops and discard garlic and bay leaf. To skillet add apples and cabbage. Blend onion, sugar, vinegar and water, flour and remaining ½ teaspoon salt. Pour over cabbage and stir to mix. Cover and simmer 5 minutes. Return chops to skillet; cover and cook 20 minutes, until chops are fork tender. Makes 4 servings.

CHILI VERDE (MEXICAN STEW)

This dish is quite different from the classic Mexican dish of the same name, but it is a very delicious adaptation. And it can be made ahead and held in the refrigerator for serving the next day.

Recipe contest entry: Jeannine Johnson, Guerneville, CA

1   lb. beef stew meat (boneless chuck, preferably)
½   lb. pork stew meat
2   large onions, chopped
6   cloves fresh garlic, minced or pressed
1   teaspoon salt *each* and powdered garlic
2   tablespoons olive oil
1   can (4 oz.) diced green chiles
3   cans (8 oz. each) tomato sauce

Cut meat into 1-inch cubes. Combine meat in pot, cover with water and add half the onion and half the garlic, salt and powered garlic. Cover and simmer gently until meat is almost fork tender. Remove cover and continue cooking until meat is tender and liquid has boiled away. Meanwhile in separate saucepan, combine olive oil, remaining onion and garlic, chiles and tomato sauce. Simmer for about 10 minutes. Pour over meat and bake for 1 hour at 350 degrees.

CABALLERO CASSEROLE

Tex-Mex cuisine is all the rage. Try this southwest version of lasagna. It's appealing as well as good eating.

Recipe contest entry: Micky Kolar, Fountain Hills, AZ

2   tablespoons cooking oil
2   cups chopped onion
1   red bell pepper, seeded and chopped
1   green bell pepper, seeded and chopped
3   cloves fresh garlic, minced
2   lb. lean ground beef
1   can (16 oz.) ready-cut tomatoes, drained
1   can (4 oz.) chopped jalapeno peppers, drained
2   tablespoons chili powder
2   teaspoon salt
½   teaspoon *each* ground cumin and oregano
¼   teaspoon ground coriander
3   corn tortillas (10-inch diameter)
½   cup shredded Longhorn Cheddar cheese
1   ripe avocado, peeled and cut into 6 slices
1   cup sour cream
2   teaspoon minced parsley

Heat oil in large, heavy skillet. Saute onion and peppers until tender. Add garlic and saute 2 minutes. Add meat and brown, breaking it up until crumbly. Add tomatoes, jalapenos and spices, mixing well, and cook over medium heat until mixture is slightly thickened, about 5 minutes. Remove from heat. Oil a round 10 x 1½ inch baking dish. Place 1 tortilla in bottom of dish, trimming to fit, if necessary. Spread ⅓ of meat mixture over tortilla. Repeat layers, ending with meat. Bake in preheated 400-degree oven 15 minutes. Sprinkle with cheese and return to oven for 5 minutes. Arrange avocado slices in sunburst pattern in center of casserole. Place spoonful of sour cream in center, sprinkle with parsley and serve with additional sour cream, if desired. Makes 6 servings.

Indispensable garlic is lauded in Gilroy, where you can buy braids, (and) sample dishes.

Sunset Magazine

Poultry

Regional Winner 1983 Recipe Contest: MRS. ROBERT SOELTER, Abilene, KS

Only three chicken breasts are used in this recipe, the skin from six is necessary to wrap the 6 stuffed half breasts. Reserve the remaining 3 whole skinned chicken breasts for use in another recipe or marinate and grill them when you prepare this recipe and freeze them to serve later.

STUFFED CHICKEN BREASTS A L'AIL

6 whole chicken breasts
3 cloves fresh garlic, minced
1½ cups Monterey Jack cheese, grated
Salt
Cracked black pepper
Nutmeg
1 jar Cara Mia marinated Brussels sprouts, drained
6 teaspoons capers
Basting Sauce (recipe below)

Carefully remove skin from 6 chicken breasts and set aside. Bone chicken breasts. (Use bones for stock and three breasts in another recipe.) Cut three chicken breasts in half. Cover chicken with piece of heavy plastic wrap and pound with wooden mallet until very thin. Combine garlic and cheese. Lightly sprinkle each chicken breast with salt and cracked black pepper. Place ¼ cup garlic/cheese mixture on each breast to within 1 inch of edge. Sprinkle with nutmeg. Cut Brussels sprouts in quarters and arrange evenly over chicken. Top with capers. Fold in sides of flattened chicken and roll to make neat packages, covering stuffing well. Wrap each breast in a chicken skin, securing with toothpicks. Grill over charcoal 30 to 40 minutes, basting with sauce. Makes 6 servings.

Basting Sauce
¾ cup dry white wine
⅜ cup olive oil
3 cloves fresh garlic, minced
½ teaspoon salt

Combine all ingredients and mix thoroughly.

Winner of Prize for Best Recipe Using Most Garlic, 1982:

HELEN McGLONE, Roseville, CA

When serving this recipe to guests, invite them into the kitchen to let them count as you place the garlic cloves around the chicken. They won't believe how sweet and delicious the cooked garlic will be until they eat it!

101 GARLIC CHICKEN

10 whole chicken breasts, split, boned and skinned
Salt and pepper
2 cups champagne
101 unpeeled cloves fresh garlic

Place chicken in ungreased baking pan, 12 x 16 or 18 inches. Sprinkle with salt and pepper and pour champagne over. Place garlic cloves around and between chicken pieces. Cover pan with foil. Bake at 350 degrees for 1½ hours. Remove chicken to large serving platter and place garlic around chicken. Tell guests to suck the garlic out of its skin, that it is deliciously sweet. Makes 20 servings.

Finalist in 1981 Recipe Contest: MARY JANE HIMEL, Palo Alto, CA

This recipe turns out best when prosciutto is used. Look for it in an Italian grocery or deli if not available at your supermarket. It adds considerable flavor. Also, be sure to keep the filo dough moist as you work with it. Keep it covered with a dampened towel.

GARLIC-CHICKEN FILO ROLLS

2 heads fresh garlic
½ cup dry white wine
½ cup water
Juice of 1 lemon
¼ teaspoon salt
1 lb. boned, skinned chicken breasts
6 sheets filo
¼ cup butter, melted
2½ oz. thinly sliced prosciutto *or* 3 slices boiled ham, halved
2 cups grated Swiss cheese

Separate garlic into cloves and drop into boiling water. Simmer 1 minute, drain and peel. Bring wine, water, lemon juice and salt to simmer in large saucepan. Add chicken and garlic. Cook at a bare simmer, turning occasionally, just until chicken is cooked. Remove chicken and continue cooking garlic until tender, then drain. Cut chicken into large chunks and divide into 6 portions. Lay out 1 filo sheet, brush half with butter and fold in half crosswise. Brush with butter again. Top with a portion of chicken and garlic cloves lightly mashed with a fork along a short end. Top with ⅙ of the prosciutto, and ⅓ cup cheese. Fold in the sides and roll up. Repeat with remaining filo sheets. Work quickly so filo doesn't dry out. Place rolls on lightly greased baking sheet and brush them with butter. Bake at 400 degrees about 20 minutes, until golden. Makes 6 rolls.

Regional Winner in 1983 Recipe Contest: EMMALEA KELLEY, Greenbelt, MD

One good way to be sure that the chicken you are preparing absorbs the flavors of the herbs and spices used in the recipe is to make a paste and rub it all over the bird between the skin and the flesh. This requires using your fingers to break the skin away from the chicken, leaving it in place, however, to hold the seasonings tightly.

KISS ME NOW—CHICKEN

2   heads fresh garlic
1   cup water
1   fryer/broiler chicken, about 3 to 4 pounds
¼   teaspoons *each* black pepper and dill weed
¼   teaspoon salad oil
¼   lb. fresh mushrooms, rinsed and trimmed
6   pieces of celery, 1 inch each
2   tablespoons flour
1   tablespoon cooking sherry
1   cup half-and-half

Separate garlic cloves and discard loose skin, but do not peel. Boil garlic in water in small saucepan for 30 minutes. Meanwhile, entering from both the neck section and rear of the chicken, break the membranes which attach the skin to the body of the chicken with the index finger. Remove all fat from chicken. Strain water from garlic into small bowl and reserve. Scatter garlic on plate to cool. Press each clove from the pointed end into a small bowl. Discard skins. Preheat oven to 350 degrees. Add pepper and dill to garlic paste in bowl and blend well. Spoon half the mixture under the skin of the chicken, patting gently to distribute evenly. Spread remainder of garlic mixture inside chicken. Place chicken in lightly oiled shallow baking dish and fill cavity with mushrooms. Arrange celery around chicken. Bake at 350 degrees for 1½ hours, basting every 15 minutes with reserved garlic liquid. Remove chicken to serving dish. Remove mushrooms and chop. Discard celery. Scrape drippings from baking dish into small pan. Stir flour in pan drippings. Add mushrooms, sherry and half-and-half. Bring to a boil, stirring constantly. Turn heat off and stil until well thickened. Quarter chicken and serve with sauce and hot cornbread or biscuits, rice, pasta, potatoes or grits. Makes 4 servings.

Finalist in 1984 Recipe Contest: JAN E. SHELTON, Escondido, CA

In this recipe chicken breasts are browned in butter and then baked covered with a garlic cream sauce. When done they are beautifully presented garnished with colorful slices of California avocado and mandarin oranges.

CALIFORNIA CHICKEN

60 cloves fresh garlic (about
    5 heads)
    Boiling water
 3 cups whipping cream
    Salt and white pepper to
    taste
¼ cup butter
 4 whole chicken breasts,
    split, skinned and boned
⅛ teaspoon *each* cinnamon
    and dried tarragon
 2 ripe avocados
    Juice of 1 lime
 1 small can (6 oz.) mandarin
    orange slices, drained
 1 tablespoon chopped fresh
    parsley
    Paprika

Place garlic cloves in a saucepan with boiling water to cover. Boil for 2 minutes. Drain, then peel cloves. Return garlic to pan and add whipping cream. Simmer, stirring occasionally, until garlic is very tender and cream is thickened and reduced by half. Rub garlic and cream through a wire sieve. Return to saucepan and season with salt and pepper. Set aside and place plastic wrap on cream surface. Heat butter in frying pan over medium high heat. Add chicken and saute for 1 minute, turning chicken once. Do not brown. Place chicken in ovenproof platter. Bake in 325-degree oven 7 to 10 minutes. Meanwhile peel avocados, cut into ½-inch slices and toss with lime juice. Pour garlic mixture over chicken and return to oven for 2 or 3 minutes. Garnish with drained avocado and orange slices. Sprinkle with chopped fresh parsley and paprika to taste. Serve at once. Makes 4 to 6 servings.

Garlic. It's the clove with clout.

Miami News

Finalist in 1983 Recipe Contest: STACEY HAROLDSEN, Los Angeles, CA

Though not a winner, this tasty recipe was popular with the judges who thought the combination of garlic, peppers and balsamic vinegar made a wonderful sauce for the chicken. The fresh basil is an important ingredient also, but if not available dried basil can be substituted.

CHICKEN PEPERONATA

2 whole chickens, about 3 lb. each
2 tablespoons butter
2 whole heads fresh garlic
Salt and pepper
2 large sprigs fresh rosemary
3 large green bell peppers
3 large red bell peppers
¼ cup pine nuts
¼ cup extra virgin olive oil
¼ cup Italian balsamic vinegar
1 tablespoon sugar
3 tablespoons chopped fresh basil
Lettuce leaves and basil springs for garnish

Preheat oven to 375 degrees. Wash chickens and pat dry; rub with butter. Separate cloves of garlic but do not peel. Sprinkle cavities of chickens with salt and pepper; place a sprig of rosemary and half of the garlic cloves in each. Roast breast-side down for 1 hour, then turn breast-side up and continue roasting until tender, about 15 minutes. Remove from oven when cool enough to handle, remove meat from bones, pulling the meat into strips. Reserve cooked garlic cloves. Broil peppers until skins are charred, then hold under running water while removing skins and seeds. Cut half the peppers into strips and reserve the rest. Remove skins from 6 of the cooked garlic cloves and mince finely. Toast pine nuts in a dry skillet over medium heat. Combine olive oil, vinegar and sugar in a bowl. Toss chicken, peppers, pine nuts, basil, minced garlic and dressing. Add salt and pepper to taste. Line serving platter with lettuce and mound chicken salad on top. Garnish with the reserved peppers, the cooked garlic cloves (skins and all) and basil sprigs. Serve at room temperature. Makes 6 to 8 servings.

Finalist in 1984 Recipe Contest: CINDY NEVA, Acton, CA

Yum. Yum. This dish is good and spicy and at its best when the chicken is allowed to marinate overnight in the refrigerator.

SPICY GARLIC CHICKEN

1 **bunch cilantro WITH ROOTS**
1 **large whole head fresh garlic, peeled**
2 **tablespoons coarse black pepper**
1 **teaspoon ground curry powder**
¼ **teaspoon crushed red chile pepper**
¼ **cup peanut oil**
⅓ **cup soy sauce**
1 **whole chicken or 12 drumsticks, wings or thighs Sweet Garlic Sauce for Dipping (recipe below)**

Cut roots off cilantro and place with garlic, some cilantro leaves and a few stems in food processor and whirl until coarsely chopped, or chop by hand. Turn mixture into bowl, add remaining whole cilantro leaves, pepper, curry powder, chili pepper, peanut oil and soy sauce. Mix well. Pour mixture over chicken and marinate 4 hours or as long as overnight. Meanwhile prepare Sweet Garlic Sauce for Dipping. Barbecue chicken over low glowing coals about 1 hour, basting occasionally and turning chicken several times. Serve with Sweet Garlic Sauce for Dipping. Makes 4 servings.

Sweet Garlic Sauce for Dipping
3 **cups sugar**
1 **cup vinegar**
2 **tablespoons coarse black pepper**
1 **teaspoon dry red chile pepper**
½ **teaspoon salt**
1 **drop red food coloring**
1 **whole head fresh garlic, peeled and chopped**

In 2-quart saucepan bring sugar and vinegar to boil. Add pepper, chile pepper, salt and food coloring. Boil 5 minutes, stirring to prevent sticking. (Be careful not to permit mixture to boil over pan.) Remove from heat and stir in chopped garlic. Refrigerate.

. . . Garlic Chicken . . . the memory sounded a chorus of angels' trumpets in my stomach.

TWA Ambassador

SHANGHAI CHICKEN ON SHANGHAI RICE

For a potluck or to prepare this Oriental chicken dish in advance, bone chicken after it cools and combine chicken and sauce with rice in a casserole, then reheat before serving.

Recipe contest entry: John J. Moon, San Francisco, CA

4 tablespoons oil or butter or combination
12 medium onions, sliced
   Freshly ground pepper
1 tablespoons soy sauce
8 chicken thighs
¼ cup grated ginger root, or more if desired
16 cloves fresh garlic, minced, or more if desired
½ cup oyster sauce
2 tablespoons Worcestershire sauce

Heat oil or butter in large skillet over medium heat, add onions and pepper and saute until onions are golden. Stir in soy sauce. Add chicken, skin side down with skin touching skillet, and continue cooking. While skin browns, top chicken with equal amounts of grated ginger and minced garlic. Turn chicken over so that garlic and ginger are underneath and continue cooking, lowering heat if necessary to prevent burning. Cover chicken with onions and allow to cook for about 10 minutes more. Turn chicken again and top each thigh with oyster sauce. Cook for 5 minutes more and turn chicken again. Cook 5 minute, turn chicken and add Worcestershire sauce, stirring into onions. Continue cooking until chicken is thoroughly browned and onions have reduced to form a sauce. Total cooking time is approximately 1 hours.

Shanghai Rice
1 cup rice
½ lb. ham, cut into small chunks
1 cup peas, fresh or frozen
   Small chunks of peeled ginger root (optional)

Prepare rice according to package directions. Cook the ham, peas and optional ginger in with the rice. Serve chicken over rice. Makes 4 to 6 servings.

WILD RICE AND CHICKEN

Wild rice, which is not a rice at all but the grain of a tall, aquatic North American grass, is a true delicacy. It is prepared like ordinary rice, but takes a little longer to cook. It should maintain a bit of a chewy quality to be really good.

Recipe contest entry: M. Shipman, San Francisco, CA

1	cup uncooked wild rice
2¼	cups chicken broth
8	to 10 cloves fresh garlic, minced or pressed
2	tablespoons soy sauce
2	teaspoons poultry seasoning
	Coarsely ground black pepper
½	pound mushrooms, sliced
1	green bell pepper, chopped
6	stalks of celery, chopped
6	half chicken breasts, boned and skinned
	Chopped green onions for garnish

Rinse rice well at least 3 times. In casserole, place chicken broth, garlic, soy sauce, poultry seasoning and black pepper. Stir. Then add rice, mushrooms, bell pepper and celery. Mix well. "Bury" chicken in rice-vegetable mixture. Cover and bake at 350 degrees for 1 hour. Remove from heat and let stand for ½ hour with cover still on. Garnish with sliced green onions and serve. Makes 6 servings.

CHICKEN ALLA TOSCANO

This chicken entree can be made ahead in a large baking dish, covered with foil and refrigerated until ready to bake. May take slightly longer to cook if cold when placed in the oven.

Recipe contest entry: Carole A. Lake, Gilroy, CA

3	to 3½ lb. frying chicken, cut in serving pieces
	Flour
	Cooking oil
6	cloves fresh garlic, minced
3	medium leaves fresh basil, chopped fine
½	cup chopped fresh parsley
1	can (5 oz.) button mushrooms, drained
¼	cup butter
⅓	cup dry white wine
	Salt and pepper to taste
	Fresh parsley sprigs for garnish (optional)

Dredge chicken in flour and brown in oil over medium heat. Place browned chicken in large baking dish and set aside. Saute garlic, basil and parsley in butter. Drizzle evenly over chicken. Slowly pour wine and mushrooms over. Salt and pepper lightly; cover with foil and bake at 350 degrees for 40 minutes or until done. Garnish with parsley sprigs if desired. Makes 4 servings.

GARLIC CHICKEN WITH PLUM SAUCE

Here are two recipes in one. the pickled garlic that is one of the main ingredients must be made at least 1 month before you prepare the chicken dish. Be sure to make several batches. Pickled garlic is an outstanding condiment.

Recipe contest entry: Kathleen McElroy, Madison, WI

Pickled Garlic

Put 2 or 3 heads of garlic, separated into cloves but unpeeled, into a small jar with tightly fitting lid. Add white vinegar and sugar to cover, adding ½ teaspoon sugar for each ½ cup vinegar. Refrigerate 1 month before using. Keeps indefinitely.

Garlic Chicken

- 1 chicken breast, skinned, boned and partially frozen for easy slicing
- 2 tablespoons Chinese plum sauce
- 1 tablespoon Japanese soy sauce
- 1 tablespoon cornstarch
- 1½ teaspoon pickled garlic vinegar
- 6 to 8 large dried Chinese mushrooms
- 2 scallions or green onions
- 4 large cloves pickled garlic
- 2 thin slices fresh ginger
- 3 tablespoons vegetable oil

Slice chicken breast thin and mix with 1 tablespoon plum sauce, soy sauce, cornstarch and pickled garlic vinegar. Let sit for ½ hour. Meanwhile, soak mushrooms in lukewarm water for ½ hour. Squeeze dry, cut out tough center stem and slice into thin strips. Split scallions lengthwise and shred into 1-inch lengths. Peel pickled garlic and mince. Chop ginger fine. Heat oil in wok or heavy skillet over high heat. Stir garlic and ginger in hot oil until they begin to brown. Add marinated chicken and stir until cooked through. Remove chicken and add remaining 1 tablespoon cooking oil. Quickly stir scallions, mushrooms and remaining 1 tablespoon plum sauce in oil until vegetables are wilted. Return chicken to mixture and stir until heated through. Serve with rice. Makes 2 servings.

OYSTER SAUCE TURKEY BREAST WITH PEAS AND MUSHROOMS

Although this recipe could be made with soy sauce as a substitute for the oyster sauce, the dish has a much richer flavor made with the latter. Available in the Oriental section of most supermarkets, oyster sauce is a concentrated concoction of oysters cooked in soy sauce and brine.

Recipe contest entry: Cecilly Jacobsen, Fallon, NV

1½ lb. boned turkey breast
2 tablespoons vegetable oil
4 large cloves fresh garlic, peeled and minced
1 piece fresh ginger, 2 inches long, peeled and minced
½ cup chicken stock or bouillon
4 tablespoons oyster sauce
1 tablespoon *each* soy sauce and sherry
1 teaspoon sugar
1 pkg. (10 oz.) frozen green peas
1 can (4 oz.) button mushrooms, drained
2 teaspoons cornstarch mixed with 2 teaspoons water
1 green onion, chopped fine

Cut turkey into 1-inch cubes. Heat oil in wok or skillet; add garlic and ginger and stir-fry, being careful not to burn garlic. Add turkey and stir-fry to brown lightly. Mix chicken stock, oyster sauce, soy sauce, sherry and sugar and pour over turkey, stirring to coat turkey well. Cover and reduce heat; simmer for about 5 minutes. Stir in peas and mushrooms and stir until heated through, about 2 minutes. Stir cornstarch mixture and add to turkey. Cook, stirring, until mixture thickens slightly. Serve sprinkled with green onions. Makes 6 serving.

WOKING GARLIC CHICKEN

The slightly Oriental touch in the recipe has great appeal, especially for kids. If you don't have a wok, use a large skillet or electric frying pan.

Recipe contest entry: Marlene Sasaki Jose, Los Angeles

3 large dried shiitake mushrooms
1 lb. diced boned chicken breast
1 tablespoon dry white wine
¼ teaspoon *each* salt and pepper
1 can (14½ oz.) chicken broth
¼ cup tomato paste
2 tablespoons cornstarch
2 tablespoons brandy
Salt and pepper to taste
2 tablespoons peanut oil
1 whole head fresh garlic, peeled and sliced
1 large green bell pepper, seeded and julienned
1 small onion, chopped
1 can (8 oz.) water chestnuts, drained and coarsely chopped
Cilantro for garnish

Soak dried mushrooms in small bowl of hot water. Set aside for 20 minutes. Place chicken in bowl and cover with wine and salt and pepper. Set aside. Rinse soaking mushrooms, squeeze out excess water, cut stem off at base and discard. Slice mushrooms very thin. Combine broth, tomato paste, cornstarch, brandy and salt and pepper; set aside. Turn heat in wok on medium-high. Place 2 tablespoons oil in wok. When oil begins to smoke, lift and tilt wok slightly to coat cooking surface. Place chicken gently into oil and toss to stir-fry for 2 minutes or until chicken turns white with no pink showing. Remove from wok. Add 1 tablespoon oil and when it begins to smoke, add garlic, green pepper and onion. Stir-fry for 2 to 3 minutes. Add water chestnuts and mushrooms; stir-fry 1 minute. Return chicken to wok and pour sauce mixture over. Cook 5 minutes, stirring occasionally. Sauce will thicken. Serve on rice, garnished with cilantro. Makes 4 servings.

Garlic — from ancient times, it's imparted its potent powers.

Indianapolis Star

CHINESEY CHICKEN WINGS

This economical main dish can be baked a little quicker if you prefer. Try 375 degrees for 1 hour if you are in a hurry.

Recipe contest entry: Robyn Flipse, Ocean, NJ

3 to 4 lbs. chicken wings
    Salt and pepper to taste
5 tablespoons honey
4 tablespoons soy sauce
3 tablespoons brown sugar
1 tablespoon minced fresh garlic
1 teaspoon lemon juice
6 peppercorns
1 cup hot water

Cut tips from chicken wings and reserve for another use. Cut remaining wing in half at joint. Rinse chicken and pat dry. Set in ungreased, shallow baking pan in single layer. Sprinkle with salt and pepper. Mix together in a small jar the remaining ingredients; cover and shake well. Pour over wings. Cover pan with foil and bake for 2 hours at 325 degrees. Remove foil, reduce heat to 300 degrees and continue baking another 30 minutes, basting wings with drippings every 10 minutes. When wings are brown, remove and drain on paper towels. Serve hot or cold. Makes 4 to 5 servings.

HODGE-PODGE CHICKEN BAKE

This delicious dish has a slightly Oriental flavor. True garlic lovers may wish to increase the garlic in this recipe to make its flavor more dominant.

Recipe contest entry: Cynthia Kannenberg, Brown Deer, WI

2 broiler-fryer chickens, 3½ lb. each, each cut into 8 pieces
    Salt and pepper to taste
1 tablespoon paprika
1 can (1 lb. 4 oz.) pineapple chunks
1 can (8 oz.) tomato sauce
1 can (6 oz.) frozen orange juice concentrate
6 cloves fresh garlic, minced
¼ cup packed brown sugar
1 teaspoon cinnamon
½ teaspoon dry mustard
1 can (11 oz.) mandarin orange segments, drained

Sprinkle chicken on all sides with salt, pepper and paprika. Place in large 12 x 18-inch roasting pan. Drain pineapple, reserving juice. Mix 1 cup pineapple juice with tomato sauce, orange juice concentrate, garlic, sugar, cinnamon and mustard; pour over chicken. Bake at 350 degrees for about 1¼ hours, basting every 15 minutes. Add more pineapple juice if necessary. Add pineapple chunks the last 5 minutes of baking. Serve on bed of hot rice, garnished by orange segments. Makes 8 servings.

CHICKEN CURRY WITH PEACHES

Definitely a dish for company. It takes a little time to prepare, but is truly a delight.

Recipe contest entry: Karen Harmatuik, San Francisco, CA

½ cup butter
½ cup chopped onion
4 cloves fresh garlic, minced or pressed
2 teaspoons curry powder
3 teaspoons paprika
6 chicken half breasts or thighs
1 bunch broccoli, cut into pieces
1 small head cauliflower, separated into flowerets
¾ cup dry white wine
12 canned or fresh peach halves, sliced
2 cups yogurt
½ cup real mayonnaise
½ cup grated Monterey Jack cheese

Melt butter in small skillet. Add onion and garlic; saute until onion is soft. Stir in curry and paprika. Dip chicken in mixture until well coated; place in shallow baking dish. Steam broccoli and cauliflower briefly and arrange among chicken pieces. Carefully drizzle wine between chicken pieces. Cover loosely with foil and bake at 375 degrees for 30 minutes. Remove from oven and discard foil. Place peaches among chicken and vegetables. Mix yogurt and mayonnaise and spoon over chicken. Sprinkle with cheese. Place on lower rack of oven and broil for 8 to 10 minutes or until lightly browned. Makes 6 servings.

PHONY ABALONE

The longer the chicken marinates, the more it tastes like abalone! Leftover clam juice can be used to make chowder by adding celery, potato, pepper, 1 can baby clams and milk for white chowder or a little water and cut-up fresh tomatoes for red chowder. And you can change the recipe to "Unreal Veal" by adding Parmesan cheese to the bread crumbs and omitting the tartar sauce.

Recipe contest entry: Sylvia Walker, Monterey, CA

4 chicken breast halves, boned, skinned and sliced into thin steaks
1 bottle (8 oz.) clam juice
6 cloves fresh garlic, peeled and halved
2 eggs, lightly beaten
1½ cups fine bread crumbs
4 to 6 tablespoons butter
Lemon wedges
Tartar sauce (optional

Place chicken steaks between two sheets of waxed paper and pound thin. Place in flat airtight container. Pour clam juice over and add fresh garlic. Cover and refrigerate for 36 to 48 hours, turning chicken once or twice if clam juice does not cover completely. Drain chicken. Dip in beaten egg, then in bread crumbs. Saute lightly in butter. Serve with lemon wedges and tartar sauce if desired. Makes 4 servings.

CHICKEN KARMA

This is a dish for lovers of Indian cuisine as well as garlic. Some may wish to cut back a bit on the ginger.

Recipe contest entry: Elizabeth Balderston, Ramona, CA

4 tablespoons butter
1 large onion, thinly sliced
6 cloves fresh garlic, diced
1 tablespoon fresh ginger, diced
¾ teaspoon whole cumin seed
½ teaspoon *each* coriander and mustard seed
½ teaspoon crushed red chiles
3 chicken breasts, skinned, boned and cubed
3 tablespoons raw almonds, ground in electric blender
1 teaspoon turmeric
½ teaspoon salt
¼ teaspoon *each* ground cloves and cinnamon
½ cup plain yogurt
¼ cup chopped fresh cilantro
1 tablespoon lemon juice

Melt butter in large, heavy skillet or Dutch oven over medium-high heat. Cook onion, garlic and ginger until onion is tender. Add cumin, coriander seed, mustard seed and chiles; cook 2 minutes. Add chicken; stir and cook until chicken begins to turn white. Stir in almonds, turmeric, salt, cloves and cinnamon; cook another minute. Add yogurt; stir until blended, then reduce heat, cover and simmer for 1 hour. Just before serving, stir in cilantro and lemon juice. Serve over rice. Makes 4 servings.

THIRTY-CLOVE CHICKEN

Not only will this dish banish evil spirits, but it will raise good ones, we're told, especially those of garlic lovers, for it contains 30 whole cloves!

Recipe contest entry: Leah Jackson, Marshfield, MA

2 broiler-fryer chickens, cut in serving-size pieces
4 tablespoons olive oil
2 tablespoons butter
1 tablespoon flour
1 can (14½ oz.) chicken broth
30 cloves fresh garlic, peeled
1 cup rice
Fresh chives and parsley, minced

Brown chicken in 2 tablespoons oil and butter. Remove from pan and stir in flour, then broth and garlic. Bring to boil, return chicken to pan and simmer, covered, for 45 minutes. Saute rice in remaining 2 tablespoons oil until rice is opaque. Add to chicken, easing into liquid with fork. Cover and simmer another 25 minutes. Just before serving, stir in fresh herbs. Makes 8 servings.

GYPSY GARLIC CHICKEN

This is a true garlic lover's adaptation of a classic recipe which always begins: "First you steal the chicken . . . ."

Recipe contest entry: Jeanne D'Avray, Metairie, LA

21 or more cloves fresh garlic, peeled
8 chicken breast halves and 4 legs
2 tablespoons cooking oil
2 medium onions, sliced
1½ cups water
1 can (8 oz.) tomato sauce
½ cup dry sherry
2 tablespoons sugar
1 tablespoon vinegar
1 teaspoon *each* salt and chervil
2 large bay leaves
1 heaping tablespoon whole peppercorns
1 cheesecloth square, 4 x 4 inches
Lemon slices and parsley for garnish

Cut 5 garlic cloves into thin slices. With sharp pointed knife, pierce chicken skin at 1½ inch intervals and insert garlic slices between the skin and the flesh. Heat oil to medium-high and saute chicken, onions and remaining whole garlic cloves until chicken is slightly browned, being careful that onions and garlic do not burn. Stir often. Add water, tomato sauce, sherry, sugar, vinegar, salt and chervil; bring to a boil. Wrap bay leaves and peppercorns in cheese cloth and tie opposite ends to make a bag. Drop into boiling sauce; reduce heat, cover, and simmer for 25 to 30 minutes until chicken is tender. Remove spice bag. Secure a parsley sprig into center of 8 lemon slices with a toothpick. Place on top of larger pieces of meat, cover and simmer for 8 minutes. Arrange on platter, decorated with additional fresh parsley, if desired. Serve at once, accompanied by buttered noodles. Makes 8 servings.

CHICKEN AND SAUSAGE RAGOUT ALLA ROSINA

The definition of "ragout" is "a highly seasoned dish of stewed meat and vegetables." In this recipe the seasoning begins with 20 cloves of fresh garlic, the meat includes chicken and spicy Italian sausage and the vegetables, mushrooms and red peppers and the finished product is outstanding! And it's even better the next day!

Recipe contest entry: Rosina Wilson, Albany, CA

1   fryer, about 3 lb., cut into small pieces
1   lb. Italian-style fennel sausages, halved
¼   cup olive oil
1   large onion, minced
½   lb. button mushrooms
20 or more cloves fresh garlic, peeled
⅓   cup brandy
1   can (28 oz.) Italian-style plum tomatoes, chopped
2   cups red wine
3   bay leaves
½   teaspoon fennel seeds
1   roasted red pepper, cut in strips (canned may be used)
3   sprigs *each* fresh oregano and parsley
     Salt and pepper to taste
12 oz. fusilli (spiral noodles) Parmesan cheese, freshly grated

In large skillet, brown chicken and sausages in oil. Transfer to large heatproof casserole. Saute onion, mushrooms and garlic briefly in oil that remains; add brandy, then increase heat and ignite. Pour mixture, along with tomatoes, wine, bay leaves and fennel seeds into the casserole and simmer 1 hours, skimming fat frequently. Add roasted pepper, oregano and parsley; simmer 10 more minutes to blend flavors. Skim fat, add salt and pepper. Serve over fusilli which has been cooked *al dente* according to package directions. Sprinkle liberally with Parmesan cheese. Makes 4 to 6 servings.

If you face toward Gilroy and take a deep breath, you can almost smell the good times being cooked up for the weekend.

San Jose Mercury News

FRENCH GARLIC CHICKEN A LA INGRAM

This recipe was rated a "10" by our testers. What more can we say?

Recipe contest entry: Robert Ingram, Del Mar, CA

9   large fresh garlic cloves, peeled
4   tablespoons fresh lemon juice
4   chicken breasts, boned and skinned
3   tablespoons butter or margarine
1   tablespoon cooking oil
1   cup sliced mushrooms
¾   cup dry white wine
1   teaspoon salt
1   bay leaf
¾   cup chicken broth
1½ teaspoon Dijon-style mustard
1   tablespoon chopped parsley

Finely mince or press 4 cloves garlic in small dish with lemon juice. Rub mixture over chicken. Let stand 10 minutes. Meanwhile melt butter and oil over medium heat in large skillet and add chicken. Saute for 12 to 15 minutes, turning once. Add mushrooms, wine, salt and bay leaf and remaining garlic. Cover and cook for 10 to 12 minutes. Blend mustard and broth and add, cooking, covered, for 10 to 15 minutes more or until chicken is tender. Remove chicken and whole garlic cloves to platter and keep warm. Discard bay leaf. Bring pan liquids to boil and cook rapidly to reduce and thicken slightly. Pour liquids over chicken and sprinkle all lightly with parsley. Spread the garlic on bread accompanying the meal! Makes 4 servings.

CHICKEN MAUI

Pineapple slices, lichee nuts and kumquats add a touch of the Hawaiian islands to this recipe for stuffed chicken breasts.

Recipe contest entry: Barbara Cohen, Philadelphia, PA

1 lb. ground pork
1 small onion, minced
3 or more cloves fresh garlic, minced
2 scallions or green onions, chopped
2 tablespoons oil
½ cup bread crumbs
1 egg
¼ cup plus 1 tablespoon soy sauce
1 can (8 oz.) water chestnuts, drained and chopped
6 small whole chicken breasts, boned and skinned
½ cup chicken broth
1 tablespoon honey
Black pepper to taste
6 tablespoons sesame seeds
1 large can pineapple slices, (15¼ oz.) drained
1 can (11 oz.) lichee nuts, drained
1 jar (8 oz.) kumquats, drained
Curley parsley

In large skillet, saute pork, onion, garlic and scallions in oil until pork loses pinkness. Remove from heat. Add bread crumbs, egg, ¼ cup soy sauce and water chestnuts. Stuff chicken breasts with this mixture, securing with toothpicks or wooden skewers if necessary. In large baking dish, mix broth, honey, 1 tablespoon soy suace and pepper. Place chicken in pan and bake 35 minutes at 325-degrees, turning once and basting. Sprinkle with sesame seeds and top with pineapple. Broil for 3 minutes and remove to heated platter. Garnish with lichee nuts, kumquats and curly parsley. Makes 6 servings.

HERBED CHEESE AND CHICKEN IN PUFF PASTRY

A lovely main course for family and guests, this recipe is not at all difficult to prepare and makes a beautiful presentation.

Recipe contest entry: Mary Jane Himel, Palo Alto, CA

20 large cloves fresh garlic
 6 chicken thighs
2½ cups chicken broth
 9 slices bacon, fried
 5 oz. cream cheese
1½ teaspoon tarragon
 1 pkg. (10 oz.) frozen puff
   pastry patty shells,
   thawed
 1 egg, slightly beaten

Blanch garlic in boiling water 1
minute. Peel. Place with chicken and
broth in saucepan and simmer gently, covered, for 30 minutes. Remove
chicken and garlic from broth. Skin
chicken and remove bones. Place 1½
slices bacon where bones were. Puree
garlic with 3 tablespoons broth,
cream cheese and tarragon. On lightly floured board, roll out a pastry
shell into an 8-inch circle. Put a
stuffed chicken thigh on top, then 2
tablespoons garlic-cheese mixture.
Moisten edges of pastry with a finger
dipped in cold water. Gather edges at
the top and crimp to seal. Repeat
with remaining 5 shells. Place filled
pastries on lightly buttered baking
sheet. Brush tops with beaten egg
and bake at 400 degrees for 25
minutes or until golden brown. Makes
6 servings.

Garlic is a cook's best friend.
Chicago Sun-Times

SQUABS A LA SANTA CRUZ

Squab is a term used in the U.S. and Britain for a young pigeon, weighing usually no more than a pound. If not available, substitute Rock Cornish Game Hens which are available frozen at most supermarkets.

Recipe contest entry: Lisa Gorman, San Francisco, CA

2 squabs, 1 to 1¼ lb. each
6 tablespoons butter
8 cloves fresh garlic, peeled and finely chopped
1 medium tomato, peeled, seeded and finely chopped
2 tablespoons chopped parsley
Pinch of thyme
½ cup dry white wine
Garlic salt and pepper to taste
Lemon pepper and salt to taste (optional)
6 fresh mushrooms, sliced

Split squabs and remove breast bones. In skillet, sear squabs on both sides in hot butter. Add garlic, tomato, parsley and thyme. Blend well, then add wine, salt and pepper. Cover and cook over low heat about 30 minutes. Add mushrooms and continue cooking for 10 to 15 minutes until squab is tender. Serve garnished with thin slices of orange with noodles or rice. Makes 2 to 3 servings.

Seafood

Winner of 1984 Recipe Contest: BEVERLY STONE, Berkeley, CA

"To win first prize, improvise," said Beverly Stone, and improvise she did. Her recipe was developed out of necessity when she found herself with only a few ingredients in the house which, when combined, became an outstanding new garlic salsa to serve over fish. The judges agreed it was quite a catch.

GRILLED FISH WITH GARLIC SALSA

½ cup fruity olive oil
5 tablespoons lemon juice
4 cloves fresh garlic, peeled and slivered
1 bunch fresh cilantro, chopped to make ½ cup, reserving some whole leaves for garnish
   Salt and freshly ground pepper to taste
6 firm-fleshed fish fillets, about 6 oz. each and ¾ inch thick*
¼ lb. sweet butter
¼ cup chopped sweet red onion
2 small hot green chiles, finely minced
1 tablespoon finely minced fresh garlic
1 lb. ripe tomatoes, peeled and chopped
   Lemon wedges

Mix together olive oil, 4 tablespoons lemon juice, slivered garlic, ¼ cup chopped cilantro and salt and pepper to taste. Add fish fillets and marinate for 1 hour or as long as overnight. Meanwhile prepare Garlic Salsa. In a frying pan over medium heat, melt 2 tablespoons butter. Saute onion, chiles and minced garlic until soft, stirring. Add tomatoes and the remaining 1 tablespoon lemon juice. Cook, stirring, for 10 minutes. Remove from heat and add salt and pepper to taste. Stir in remaining ⅓ cup chopped cilantro. Slowly stir in remaining butter until melted. Barbecue fish over low glowing coals about 7 minutes or until done to your liking, turning fish once. Remove to warm serving platter. Top with Garlic Salsa. Garnish with lemon wedges and reserved cilantro leaves.
Makes 6 servings.

*Angler (sometimes called Monkfish) is particularly good in this recipe.

JAMBALAYA A LA CREOLE

To make Jambalaya "Santa Cruz-style" just substitute calamari for the shrimp in this recipe. Great dish for a crowd. Serve with hot cornbread or sweet French bread.

Recipe contest entry: Bruce Engelhardt, Santa Cruz, CA

1½   lb. cooked shrimp (or cooked calamari)
1   lb. smoked rope-style sausage, cut in ¼ inch slices
1   lb. ham, diced
½   cup cooking oil
½   cup flour
1   red onion, finely chopped
1   cup chopped green bell pepper
2   stalks celery, finely chopped
2   shallots, chopped
4   or more cloves fresh garlic, chopped
2   tomatoes, chopped
1   can (16 oz.) tomato sauce
1   tablespoon crushed oregano
1   teaspoon salt
½   teaspoon chopped fresh cilantro
¼   teaspoon *each* red pepper, black pepper, ground cloves, allspice and cumin
1   cup red wine
2   bay leaves
½   cup chopped parsley
1   cup hot water
2   cups long grain white rice
¼   cup chopped green onion tops for garnish
    Louisiana-style hot sauce, if desired

Clean shrimp (if using calamari, cut into strips) and set aside. Brown sausage and ham in oil; set aside. Stir in flour and cook, stirring frequently, until dark brown in color and syrupy. Add more oil or more flour, if necessary. Add one at a time the onion, celery, bell pepper, shallots and garlic, cooking each until just done before adding the next. Add tomatoes, stirring, to prevent sticking. Stir in tomato sauce, then oregano, salt, cilantro and spices, wine and bay leaves. Simmer sauce about 20 minutes until flavors are well blended. Add more wine if sauce becomes too thick. Add parsley, sausage and ham, water and raise heat to high simmer. Add rice and shrimp (if using calamari, do not add until last 5 minutes of cooking time) and reduce heat to low, cover and cook for about 20 minutes or until rice is done. Garnish with green onions and serve with Louisiana-style hot sauce for those who like extra zest. Makes 12 servings.

SUPERSONIC FISH STEW

Whether you call it stew or chowder, this dish has plenty of flavor and is very easy to prepare.

Recipe contest entry: Jacqueline McComas, Frazer, PA

2 tablespoons cooking oil
1 cup chopped onions
3 cloves fresh garlic, minced
¼ cup *each* chopped green bell pepper and celery
2 lb. seafood, cut up (scallops, shrimp, flounder etc. or mix)
1 can (10¾ oz.) condensed tomato soup, undiluted
1 can 10¾ oz.) condensed clam chowder, undiluted
1 soup can water
¼ cup dry white wine
4 tablespoons minced parsley
  Salt and pepper to taste
2 tablespoons minced chives for garnish

In large saucepan, heat oil; add onions, garlic, bell pepper and celery. Saute until vegetables are lightly cooked. Add fish, soups, water, wine, 2 tablespoons parsley and salt and pepper. Bring to boil and simmer for 20 minutes, or until fish is done. Sprinkle with remaining parsley and/or chives and serve with plenty of crusty bread. Makes 6 to 8 servings.

GARLIC CLAMS

Lots of hot sourdough French bread is a must to sop up the delicious juices!

Recipe contest entry: Roberta Robinson, Campbell, CA

12 cloves fresh garlic, minced
1 bunch green onions, minced
½ cup butter
¼ cup vegetable oil
½ cup chopped parsley
1 teaspoon Italian seasoning
1 cup *each* dry white wine, clam juice and water
24 cherrystone clams, brushed and cleaned

In large skillet, saute garlic and onion in butter and oil for 1 minutes. Add parsley and seasoning. Add wine, clam juice and water and cook 2 minutes. Now add clams and cook, covered, until clams open, about 10 to 12 minutes. Serve in bowls. Makes 2 servings.

MARINATED SQUID ALLA ROSINA

An outstanding recipe from the winner of the 1982 Recipe Contest. For best flavor, be sure to prepare this several hours before serving time.

Recipe contest entry: Rosina Wilson, Albany, CA

3 lb. squid
¼ cup olive oil
⅛ cup *each* lemon juice and red wine vinegar
1 tablespoon Dijon-style mustard
Salt and pepper to taste
1 medium purple onion, coarsely chopped
1 roasted red bell pepper, cut in strips
½ cup diagonally sliced baby carrots, lightly poached
½ cup Nicoise olives
¼ cup chopped parsley
6 cloves fresh garlic, sliced
3 tablespoons capers
1 tablespoon slivered lemon peel
Lettuce, if desired

Clean squid and cut in rings. Poach in boiling water in small batches for 30 seconds. Drain well. Prepare marinade by mixing olive oil, lemon juice, vinegar, mustard and salt and pepper. Set aside. Combine squid and remaining ingredients in large bowl and pour marinade over. Refrigerate several hours. Serve over lettuce or as an appetizer salad. Makes 8 servings.

BAKED SQUID SICILIAN

This recipe can be prepared ahead of time, refrigerated and baked just before serving.

Recipe contest entry: Kay Lucido, Hollister, CA

2 lb. squid, cleaned and drained
¼ cup vegetable oil
1 bunch parsley, chopped
1 cup toasted bread crumbs
½ cup *each* grated Parmesan and Romano cheese
3 cloves fresh garlic, minced
1 teaspoon oregano
Salt and pepper to taste

Dip squid in oil. Combine remaining ingredients. Roll oiled squid in bread crumb mixture; roll up and place on oiled jelly roll pan, cut side down. Bake in preheated 425-degree oven for 20 minutes. Makes 4 servings.

CALAMARI DEL MEDITERRANEAN

An outstanding dish, best served over fresh fettuccine or linguine with freshly grated Romano cheese.

Recipe contest entry: Karen Occhipinti, Los Gatos, CA

4 lb. calamari (squid), cleaned
1 cup plus 3 tablespoons butter
½ cup olive oil
10 cloves fresh garlic, minced
Salt and pepper to taste
⅓ cup dry white wine
1 lb small to medium fresh mushrooms, cut in quarters
3 medium ripe tomatoes, peeled and chopped
½ cup chopped fresh parsley
4 to 5 tablespoons fresh chopped basil *or* 1 teaspoon dried basil

Cut Calamari into wide strips and rings. Melt 3 tablespoons butter in large skillet; add 3 tablespoons oil, half the garlic, calamari, salt and pepper and saute for 2 minutes. Do not overcook. Drain and reserve liquid. Set calamari aside. In same skillet, melt 1 cup butter, then add remaining oil, all but 1 tablespoon garlic and wine and simme for 1 to 2 minutes. Add mushrooms, tomatoes and ¼ cup parsley. Simmer over low heat for 8 to 10 minutes. Add basil and remaining garlic. For thinner consistency, if desired, add reserved liquid. Simmer 2 minutes longer. Serve sprinkled with remaining parsley. Makes 8 servings.

SQUID GILROY FOR TWO

Serve this squid dish alone or over spaghetti with a light, fruity Zinfandel and fresh vegetables.

Recipe contest entry: Dr. E. Stoddard, Monterey, CA

2 lb. squid, cleaned and drained
3 or 4 green onions, sliced
3 large cloves fresh garlic, sliced
4 teaspoons olive oil
1 can (8 oz.) tomato sauce
½ cup red wine
½ cup chopped parsley
3 teaspoons Italian seasoning
½ cup grated Parmesan cheese

Cut squid in rings. In large skillet cook onions and garlic in oil until lightly brown, about 2 minutes. Add squid when pan is quite hot and cook approximately 10 minutes, stirring occasionally. Add tomato sauce, wine, parsley and seasoning. Simmer for 10 minutes. Sprinkle with Parmesan, stir well and leave for 1 minute to blend flavors before serving. Makes 2 servings.

DUNGENESS CRAB DIJONNAISE

Dungeness crab, usually weighing about 3 pounds, are native to the Pacific Northwest and have a distinctively sweet taste. Any crabmeat can be substituted in this recipe if Dungeness is not available. Best served over a pasta such as fettuccine.

Recipe contest entry: Norman Noakes, Corvallis, OR

1 lb. Dungeness crabmeat
4 tablespoons butter
3 cloves fresh garlic, minced
½ lb. fresh mushrooms, thinly sliced
2 tablespoons finely chopped shallots, scallions or green onions
½ cup dry white wine
½ cup whipping cream
1 tablespoon Dijon-style mustard
Salt and pepper to taste
Lemon juice to taste
Minced fresh parsley

In skillet, saute crab in butter for 3 to 4 minutes. Remove crab and keep warm. Add garlic, shallots and mushrooms. Cook for 1 minute. Deglaze pan with wine. Reduce to 2 tablespoons. Add cream and reduce until thick. Whisk in mustard. Do *not* boil. Add salt, pepper and lemon juice. Return crab to pan and toss quickly in sauce. Serve over fettuccine. Sprinkle with parsley. Makes 4 servings.

TROUT SAUTE ALLA ROSINA

Contest winner, Rosina Wilson, definitely has a way with garlic, and her recipes are always relatively easy to prepare, something other busy people will appreciate.

Recipe contest entry: Rosina Wilson, Albany, CA

4 trout, 12 oz. each
¼ cup olive oil
½ cup *each* fine cornmeal and freshly grated Parmesan cheese
¼ teaspoon salt
¼ cup butter
20 cloves fresh garlic, minced
¾ cup dry white wine
¼ cup minced parsley
4 tablespoons capers, including juice
Juice of 2 lemons
4 lemon wedges

Remove heads, tails and scales from trout. Rinse well; pat dry, then rub skin with a little of the oil. Combine cornmeal, cheese and salt in a long bowl or dish and coat trout generously with the mixture. In a large skillet, saute trout in butter and oil over medium heat for 5 minutes on each side. Add garlic to fish and stir in oil for 2 to 3 minutes. Add wine, parsley, capers and lemon juice and cook for 5 to 10 minutes more, turning once, until trout flakes when tested with fork. Spoon reduced wine sauce over the trout and serve with lemon wedges. Makes 4 servings.

ALLA TAMEN FILLET OF SOLE ROLL-UPS

The influence of the Orient can be found in this recipe—an exotic treatment for a familiar fish.

Recipe contest entry: Stella Wolf, Culver City, CA

1 lb. fillet of sole
¼ cup peanuts
6 cloves fresh garlic, peeled
4 slices fresh ginger root, about ¼ inch thick, peeled
1 tablespoon salad oil
1 tablespoon lemon
4 teaspoons sesame oil
1 pkg. (10 oz.) frozen peas
1 cup sliced fresh mushrooms (optional)
1 tablespoon *each* soy sauce and lemon juice
1 teaspoon dry mustard powder
2 tablespoon sesame seeds

Rinse sole with cold water and set aside. In blender or food processor, combine peanuts, garlic, ginger, salad oil, lemon juice and 1 teaspoon sesame oil. Spread ¼ of paste on each fillet and roll up. Arrange fish rolls in 7 x 12 x 2-inch glass baking dish, surrounded by peas and mushrooms. Blend together remaining sesame oil, soy sauce, lemon juice and mustard. Pour over fish, allowing excess to dribble down to bottom of dish. Sprinkle sesame seeds over. Cover with aluminum foil. Bake at 350 degrees for 15 to 20 minutes or until fish tests done. Serve at once. Makes 4 servings.

SHARON'S GARLIC MONKFISH

Monkfish is also called angler or lotte. It is a firm fleshed fish, which has a flavor and texture resembling lobster.

Recipe contest entry: Sharon Cordonier, San Jose, CA

2 lb. monkfish
20 large mushrooms, sliced
8 large cloves fresh garlic, chopped
3 green onions, with tops, chopped
    Salt and pepper to taste
½ lb. butter
1 cup dry white wine
3 tablespoons Worcestershire sauce

Clean monkfish and cut into chunks. In skillet, saute mushrooms, garlic, onions, salt and pepper in ¼ lb. butter for 1 minute. Add ½ cup wine and saute until vegetables are tender. Set aside. In another large skillet, melt remaining ¼ lb. butter. Add fish and fry until fish turns white. Add Worcestershire sauce and continue cooking, covered, until liquid is reduced to half. Add mushroom-garlic mixture and remaining ½ cup wine. Cook, covered, until liquid is reduced to ¼. Serve over rice, if desired. Makes 4 servings.

GARLIC SHRIMP

A very low-calorie dish which is easy to prepare and would be enjoyed by the whole family, not just the dieters.

Recipe contest entry: Gloria Park, Los Gatos, CA

2 lb. raw shrimp (about 24)
6 cloves fresh garlic, chopped
6 scallions or green onions, with tops, minced
⅓ cup chopped fresh parsley
2 teaspoons dry vermouth
½ teaspoons soy sauce
¼ teaspoon Tabasco
8 fresh mushrooms, sliced

Rinse shrimp; remove legs, leaving tails and shells intact. With sharp knife, cut through shells down the back, leaving shells on. Devein shrimp. Mix garlic, onion, parsley, vermouth, soy sauce and Tabasco and toss with shrimp. Marinate in refrigerator for about 1 hour. Add mushrooms and toss again. Cut 2 sheets of heavy duty foil 18 x 36 inches. Double each by folding to 18 x 18 inches. Divide shrimp mixture evenly between the 2 foil sheets, making single layers. Enclose shrimp with double folds on the tops and both sides of the packages so that none of the juices can escape. Place each package on a cookie sheet and bake at 400 degrees for 15 to 20 minutes, until shrimp have turned pink. Serve immediately. Makes 6 servings.

Garlic revered as food, folk remedy for millennia.

Topeka Daily Capital

ROGER'S SCAMPI

This seafood dish is equally good served over pasta or rice. It can easily be increased to serve 6.

Recipe contest entry: Roger Kirsch, San Jose, CA

1 lb. large prawns (12 to 16 per lb.)
4 tablespoons sweet butter or margarine
¼ cup olive oil
5 cloves fresh garlic, minced
⅛ teaspoon *each* sweet basil and oregano
Juice from 1 lemon
Salt and pepper to taste
¼ cup Triple Sec or Cointreau

Shell and devein prawns; rinse and drain. Melt butter in medium skillet; add olive oil, garlic, basil and oregano and lemon juice. Saute for 1 minute. Add prawns and cook until pink. Add salt and pepper and Triple Sec and cook on high until liquid is reduced by ¾. Serve over pasta or rice. Makes 2 to 3 servings.

GARLIC SHRIMP AU GRATIN

This dish is simplicity itself, requiring only a few ingredients and a few minutes of preparation time.

Recipe courtesy of Fresh Garlic Association

2 lb. raw shrimp
1½ sticks butter (¾ cup)
2 cups fine dry bread crumbs
½ cup finely chopped parsley
4 cloves fresh garlic, minced or pressed
Salt and pepper to taste
1 cup dry sherry

Shell and devein shrimp. Toss into boiling water, return to boil and cook for about 2 minutes until shrimp turn all pink. Drain. In large skillet melt 1 stick butter (½ cup) over low heat. Add bread crumbs, parsley, garlic and salt and pepper. Stir a few minutes over low heat; pour in sherry and cook 1 minute more. Place alternate layers of shrimp and bread crumbs in well-buttered gratin dish, ending with bread crumbs. Dot with remaining butter. Bake at 350 degrees for 10 to 15 minutes. Makes 4 servings.

GARLIC SCALLOP SAUTE

A very simple dish with elegance and good flavor.

Recipe contest entry: Anne McDonald, Morgan Hill, CA

1 lb. scallops
¾ cup milk or enough to cover
⅓ cup flour
4 tablespoons *each* butter and cooking oil
4 cloves fresh garlic, minced
10 fresh mushrooms, thinly sliced
2 shallots, chopped (about 3 tablespoons)
1 teaspoons lemon juice
 Sherry

Wash scallops well to remove sand. Place in small bowl and cover with milk. Let stand for 10 minutes. Drain well and coat with flour. Shake off excess flour and set aside. Melt butter in large skillet, add oil and half the garlic and cook a few seconds. Add mushrooms, shallots and remaining garlic. Stir constantly until done. Add scallops and lemon juice; cook for 2 to 3 minutes, stirring occasionally, until scallops are just done. Remove scallops to serving platter and keep warm. Add a dash of sherry and deglaze the pan. Pour over scallops and serve. Makes 4 servings.

SCALLOPS IN GARLIC MUSHROOM SAUCE

When preparing scallops it is extremely important not to overcook them as they can become quite tough and chewy. They are best when cooked until just barely done or even slightly undercooked.

Recipe courtesy of the Fresh Garlic Association

1 lb. scallops
1 tablespoons vegetable oil
4 cloves fresh garlic, minced
1 can (5 oz.) water chestnuts, drained and sliced
2 tablespoons cornstarch mixed with 2 tablespoons water
1 teaspoon salt
⅛ teaspoon white pepper
1 cup sliced fresh mushrooms
⅓ cup sliced green onions, including stems

Place scallops in 2 quarts lightly salted water. Bring to a boil. Drain immediately. Heat vegetable oil in wok. Add garlic and stir-fry until golden. Add water chestnuts, soy, cornstarch mixture, salt and pepper and mix. Add scallops and mushrooms and cook, stirring gently, until sauce thickens and coats scallops. Remove to platter. Sprinkle with sliced green onion. Makes 2 to 3 servings.

HELEN'S SEAFOOD TREAT

Fresh shrimp and crabmeat baked in individual casseroles with a rich and buttery garlic sauce.

Recipe contest entry: Helen Cairns, Marblehead, MA

1½ lb. fresh shrimp
8 cups water
3 cloves fresh garlic, chopped
1 onion, quartered
1 bay leaf
8 tablespoons butter
1 teaspoon lemon juice
¾ cup cracker crumbs
½ lb. fresh crabmeat, lobster, scallops or other seafood
Lemon wedges and fresh parsley for garnish

Clean shrimp. Boil in water with 1 clove garlic, onion and bay leaf for 5 minutes. Drain. Melt butter in skillet; add remaining garlic and lemon juice. Add half the garlic butter to cracker crumbs. Mix well and set aside. Place shrimp and crabmeat in 4 individual casseroles. Pour remaining garlic butter evenly over seafood. Sprinkle with cracker crumbs and bake at 400 degrees for 5 minute. Serve piping hot garnished and lemon wedges and parsley. Makes 4 servings.

Miscellaneous

Finalist in 1982 Recipe Contest   LEONA PEARCE, Carmichael, CA

This recipe for a split loaf of French bread, stuffed with artichoke hearts, cheese, sour cream, olives and garlic makes 8 generous servings of crusty, cheesy, garlicky goodness.

CALIFORNIA GOURMET GARLIC LOAF

1 (1 lb.) long loaf sweet French bread
½ cup butter
6 cloves fresh garlic, crushed
1½ cups sour cream
2 cups cubed Monterey Jack cheese
¼ cup grated Parmesan cheese
2 tablespoons dried parsley flakes
2 teaspoons lemon pepper seasoning
1 can (14 oz.) artichoke hearts, drained
1 shredded Cheddar cheese
1 can (6 oz.) pitted ripe olives
Tomato slices and parsley sprigs for garnish

Cut French bread in halves lengthwise. Place halves on aluminum foil covered baking sheet. Tear out soft inner portion of bread in large chunks, leaving crusts intact. Melt butter in large skillet and stir in garlic and sesame seeds. Add bread chunks and fry until bread is golden and butter is absorbed. Remove from heat. Combine sour cream, Jack cheese, Parmesan cheese, parsley flakes and lemon pepper seasoning. Stir in drained artichoke hearts and toasted bread mixture; mix well. Spoon into bread crust shells and sprinkle with Cheddar cheese. Bake at 350 degrees for 30 minutes. Meanwhile, drain olives well. Remove bread from oven and arrange olives around edges of bread and tomato slices and parsley sprigs down center. Makes 8 servings.

Finalist in 1983 Recipe Contest: JOHN KEITH DRUMMOND, San Francisco, CA

Cooking the garlic until it is soft changes its flavor from pungent to sweet and nut-like — a very good addition to pancakes and a pleasant complement to the smokiness of the ham sauce. Serve for breakfast, brunch, lunch or even a light supper.

GARLIC PANCAKES WITH HAM SAUCE

½ lb. butter
3 tablespoons rubbed sage
3 large heads fresh garlic
2 cups self-rising flour
2 eggs
2 tablespoons oil
3½ cups milk
9 large cloves fresh garlic, minced
1 lb. lean ham, minced

Mix together 12 tablespoons (1½ sticks) butter and sage; reserve. Remove as much outer skin from garlic as possible without piercing the cloves' covering. Set garlic in saucepan, cover with water and boil gently about 45 minutes or until cloves are quite soft. Remove from heat. When cool enough to handle squeeze each clove to remove cooked garlic by grasping clove at the tip and pulling down toward base. In mixing bowl, beat garlic with fork until smooth. Add to garlic about same amount (at least 1 cup) flour, eggs, oil and 1½ cups milk to make pancake batter. Add minced garlic to batter and set aside. Melt remaining 4 tablespoons butter and keep warm. While waiting for batter to work, place half the sage butter (6 tablespoons) in saucepan, add 6 tablespoons flour to make a roux and cook at medium temperature, stirring frequently, to brown. Meanwhile in skillet, place 2 tablespoons of remaining sage butter and add ham. Heat through, but do not burn. When roux is nicely browned, add remaining 2 cups milk. Allow to thicken, stirring frequently. Add ham and skillet drippings and mix to make ham sauce. Keep warm. Heat griddle or clean skillet and grease lightly with a bit of remaining sage butter. Drop batter by spoonfuls onto griddle to make silver dollar-size pancakes. Serve with melted butter and ham sauce. Makes 2 dozen pancakes.

Regional Winner in 1981 Recipe Contest   MRS. DOMENI ROMANO, Fresno, CA

Italians are great users of garlic in their cooking. Mrs. Romano has developed this recipe not only for own use but to give as a small gift to friends and relatives who are also creative cooks.

SAVORY ITALIAN SEASONING SALT

4 whole dried red chile peppers
¼ cup dehydrated minced garlic
½ cup dehydrated minced onion
¼ cup dried oregano leaves
¼ cup dried basil leaves
¼ cup dried parsley leaves
¼ cup salt
2 tablespoons dried rosemary (optional)

With blender turned on at low speed, add ingredients in order listed. Cover and turn on high speed to pulverize and blend well. Store in shaker container with tight lid. Use for seasoning steaks, roasts, vegetables, soups, stews and salads, adding seasoning to suit taste. Makes about 1 cup.

Three nickles will get you on the subway, but garlic will get you a seat.

New York Yiddish saying

Finalist in 1984 Recipe Contest MICHELE SCIORTINO, San Diego, CA

Cookies made with garlic? Well, why not? Everyone who tasted them agreed they were delicious and would even be better with more garlic!

GARLIC CHIP COOKIES

10 cloves fresh garlic
   Boiling water
½ cup maple syrup
1 cup butter, softened
¾ cup brown sugar
¾ cup sugar
2 eggs
1 teaspoon vanilla
½ teaspoon salt
2¼ cups chocolate chips
½ cup chopped nuts
2½ cups flour
1 teaspoon baking soda

Drop garlic cloves into boiling water for about 5 minutes until tender. Peel and chop garlic and soak in maple syrup for 20 minutes. Meanwhile, cream butter, sugars, eggs and vanilla together until light and fluffy. Combine flour, baking soda and salt. Add to cream mixture. Then stir in chocolate chips and nuts. Drain garlic and add to cookie batter. Blend well. Drop cookie batter by tablespoons onto ungreased cookie sheet about 2 inches apart. Bake at 375 degrees for 8 to 10 minutes, until lightly browned. Remove from oven and cool on racks. Yield: 5 dozen cookies.

OUR BEST WURST

This homemade salami recipe makes 4 pounds, enough for 50 people when sliced as a snack. Freezes well for later use.

Recipe contest entry: Bob and Sylvia Solterbeck, Hooks, TX

10 jalapeno peppers, minced (optional)
5 cloves fresh garlic, minced
¼ cup curing salt
4 tablespoons dry red wine
2 tablespoons brown sugar
1 tablespoon *each* chili powder, Italian seasoning and coarse ground black pepper
1 teaspoon *each* ground cumin and oregano
5 lb. lean ground beef

Combine all ingredients except beef thoroughly, then mix into beef. Refrigerate mixture for 24 hours to allow flavors to mingle. Form into 4 rolls. Wrap in aluminum foil and bake in 225-degree oven for 4 hours, turning every hour. Remove foil and place on broilpan or rack to allow excess liquid to drain. Then rewrap and refrigerate or freeze. Makes 4 1-lb. salamis. Recipe may be doubled if desired.

GARLIC PIE

An attractive, well seasoned and hearty dish which can be made ahead and baked just before serving.

Recipe contest entry: Kenneth Poppa, Gilroy, CA

8 medium red potatoes, cooked
3 medium white onions, chopped
15 cloves fresh garlic, minced
3 to 4 tablespoons butter
½ teaspoon garlic salt
1 lb. Italian sausage, removed from casings
1½ tablespoon oregano
1 tablespoon cumin
Salt and pepper to taste
2 eggs
1 cup milk
6 oz. Mozzarella cheese, sliced
Paprika

Peel potatoes, reserving skins, and slice. Over low heat in covered pan, cook onion and garlic in 2 to 3 tablespoons butter for about 20 minutes. In a buttered 11-inch pie pan make a crust out of the potato skins by pressing skins firmly into pan. Sprinkle with garlic salt and dot with butter. Add sausage to onion-garlic mixture and brown. Add oregano, cumin and salt and pepper and pour into pie crust. Beat eggs and milk together lightly and pour over sausage. Top with cheese and then arrange sliced potatoes on top to form top crust. Dot with butter, sprinkle with paprika and bake in 450-degree oven for 20 to 30 minutes until heated through and top is browned. Makes 6 to 8 servings.

STEAK SAUCE ELIZABETH

This mushroom sauce is delicious over grilled steak.

Recipe contest entry: Darlene Perrin, San Jose, CA

1 medium red onion, chopped
4 cloves fresh garlic, minced or pressed
3 tablespoons olive oil
2 tablespoons butter
1 teaspoon sweet basil
½ teaspoon salt
½ cup beef broth
2 tablespoons flour mixed with water to make thin paste
1 lb. fresh mushrooms sliced

Saute onion and garlic in oil and butter with basil and salt until onion is tender. Add broth and bring to boil. Reduce heat and add flour mixture. Stir until sauce thickens. Add mushrooms and cook until tender. Do not overcook. Serve over grilled steak. Makes enough for 4 servings.

HAPPY HEART GARLIC "CHEESE" PIE WITH GARLIC-TOMATO SAUCE

Here's a recipe for those on a low-fat, low-cholesterol diet. Not only does the garlic add great flavor it has also been credited by some in the medical community with lowering cholesterol in the blood.

Recipe contest entry: Carol Granaldi, Sacramento, CA

2 egg whites
1 teaspoon fresh lemon
   juice
1 pkg. (14 oz.) firm tofu,
   mashed well
1 cup chopped onion
4 tablespoons safflower oil
½ cup chopped cooked
   mushrooms *or* 1 can (8
   oz.), drained
⅓ cup minced fresh parsley
¼ cup dry bread crumbs
6 cloves fresh garlic,
   minced
½ teaspoon-plus a pinch of
   dried oregano
   Salt and pepper to taste
1 can (1 lb.) crushed
   tomatoes
½ teaspoon crushed dried
   basil
   Dash cayenne pepper

In large mixing bowl, beat egg whites until foamy; add lemon juice and tofu. Stir well. Saute onion in 2 tablespoons oil until golden brown. Add to tofu mixture along with mushrooms, parsley, bread crumbs, half the garlic, pinch of oregano and salt and pepper to taste. Stir to mix thoroughly. Spray 8-inch glass pie plate with low-fat, no cholesterol pan spray. Pour mixture in and spread evenly. Bake at 350 degrees for 30 to 40 minutes until lightly golden in color or knife inserted in center comes out clean. Remove and let cool about 10 minutes. Meanwhile prepare sauce. Saute remaining garlic in 2 tablespoons oil until golden, then add tomatoes, ½ teaspoon oregano, basil, cayenne and salt and pepper to taste. Stir well, and bring to bubbling. Reduce heat and simmer for about 15 minutes. Cut pie into 4 wedges and top each with sauce. Makes 4 servings.

MUSHROOM CRUST FLORENTINE PIE

Crumb crust with a difference! . . . . sauteed mushrooms! Real garlic devotees will want to add more of their flavorite flavoring and yogurt could be substituted for the mayonnaise for a slightly different flavor.

Recipe contest entry: Jamie Schulte, Indianapolis, IN

½ lb. fresh mushrooms, chopped
3 tablespoons margarine
½ cup dry bread crumbs or cracker crumbs
1½ cups shredded Swiss cheese
3 tablespoons flour
1 pkg. (10 oz.) frozen chopped spinach, thawed and drained
6 crisp cooked bacon slices, crumbled
3 eggs
3 cloves fresh garlic, minced
3 scallions with tops, chopped
⅔ cup real mayonnaise
1 teaspoon parsley
½ teaspoon pepper
Cherry tomatoes and hard-cooked egg slices for garnish
Parmesan cheese

Saute mushrooms in margarine, stir in bread crumbs and press evenly in greased 9-inch pie pan over bottom and sides to form crust. Toss cheese with flour and add remaining ingredients. Mix well and fill crust with mixture. Bake at 350 degrees for about 40 minutes. Garnish as desired and sprinkle lightly with Parmesan. Makes 4 servings.

MARIE'S AIOLI

This pungent mayonnaise can be used as a dip or salad dressing or to dollop on raw oysters, steak tartare or seviche.

Recipe contest entry: Marie Spence, El Paso, TX

2 tablespoons fine dry bread crumbs
2 tablespoons wine vinegar
6 cloves fresh garlic, minced
3 egg yolks
½ teaspoon salt
Pinch of white pepper
½ cup olive oil
1 tablespoon lemon juice

Soak crumbs in vinegar; drain. Mash crumbs and garlic to a smooth paste, preferably in a mortar and pestle. Beat in yolks one at a time with salt and pepper. Then, beating vigorously, add ¼ cup olive oil, a few drops at a time. Continuing to beat, mix in the remaining oil by teaspoonfuls. Add lemon juice and mix thoroughly. Makes about 1 cup.

PATRICIA'S MARINADE

A "super good" marinade for meat or poultry.

Recipe contest entry: Patricia Canova, S. Weymouth, MA

½ cup soy sauce
¼ cup salad oil
6 cloves fresh garlic, minced
2 tablespoons honey
2 teaspoons dry mustard

Mix all ingredients together and use as marinade for meat or poultry. Makes about 1 cup.

DAVID'S PRESERVED PEPPERS

Chill before serving. These garlic peppers are absolutely irresistible and a great addition to appetizers, salads, antipasto plates or just for nibbling. Green bell peppers can be used if red peppers are not available, but the color is not as attractive.

Recipe contest entry: David Martin, Gilroy, CA

4 quarts water
6 tablespoons salt
2 cups white distilled vinegar
8 to 9 lb. red bell peppers
25 whole black peppercorns
15 cloves fresh garlic, peeled and halved
5 sprigs fresh dill
5 bay leaves

Boil water in large pot with salt until dissolved. Remove from heat and add vinegar. Cut peppers in half lengthwise, remove seeds and cut in ½ inch thick strips. Into 5 1-quart cleaned, washed canning jars place 5 whole peppercorns, 6 halves of garlic, a sprig dill and 1 bay leaf. Fill jars with pepper strips, pour brine over to about ¼ inch from the top of jar. Scald lid under boiling water and seal jar as lid manufacturer directs. Preserve peppers by water bath method. Place jars in deep kettle with rack and add boiling water to cover. Do not pour water directly on jars as they may crack. Cover kettle, heat water to boiling and boil gently for about 10 minutes, reducing heat if necessary. Remove jars from water bath and place upright on newspapers to cool. Store in cool place for at least 2 weeks prior to serving. Best served chilled. Makes 5 quarts.

CREPES POULE A LA GARLIC

A little time consuming, but well worth the effort. For extra garlic flavor, be sure to have some garlic oil on hand to add to the crepe batter. Just add a few cloves of peeled fresh garlic to a bottle of vegetable oil a few days before you decide to prepare this recipe. You'll find it good for other uses too.

Recipe contest entry: Marty Tielemans, Gilroy, CA

Veloute Sauce

- ⅓ cup butter
- 3½ tablespoons flour
- 1 cup chicken broth

Melt butter; stir in flour, cook over medium heat until golden in color. Gradually stir in broth. Cook, stirring, until thick. Set aside.

Filling

- ¼ lb. mushrooms, sliced
- 2 tablespoons butter
- 1 cup cooked chicken chunks
- 6 cloves garlic, finely chopped
- 2 tablespoons chopped green onion
- 1 tablespoon sherry
- ½ teaspoon salt
- 3 dashes Tabasco
- ⅓ cup Veloute Sauce (above)

Brown mushrooms in butter. Add chicken, garlic, onion, sherry, salt and Tabasco. Mix well. Add Veloute Sauce to moisten.

Crepes

- 4 eggs
- 1½ cups milk
- 1 cup sifted flour
- ¼ cup sherry
- 2 teaspoons garlic-flavored oil
- 1 dash salt
- 1 dash nutmeg

Blend all ingredients and cook crepes in crepe pan or on hot buttered griddle. Use about 2 tablespoons batter for each crepe.

Topping for Crepes

- 1 cup Veloute Sauce
- ½ cup whipping cream
- 1 beaten egg yolk
- ¼ cup butter
- 1 cup grated Romano cheese
- 2 teaspoons paprika

Place remaining Veloute Sauce in pan; add cream and stir until smooth. Add egg and butter.

Assemble crepes by placing equal amounts of chicken filling across center of each crepe and roll up. Place rolled side down in shallow baking pan. Cover with topping; sprinkle with cheese and paprika. Broil until golden brown.

RON'S DELUXE GARLIC SANDWICH

The ultimate comfort food!

Recipe contest entry: Ronald Dobbins, Sacramento, CA

2 tablespoons crunchy peanut butter
2 slices wheat or other bread
3 to 4 cloves fresh garlic, sliced
2 tablespoons Marie's Ranch Dressing

Spread peanut butter on one slice of bread. Place garlic slices on peanut butter and cover with remaining slice of bread which has been spread with Ranch Dressing. Makes 1 serving. "Enjoy," says Mr. Dobbins.

GARLIC POPCORN BALLS

Devilishly delicious, these are a great snack to accompany beer and football.

Recipe contest entry: Linda Tarvin, Morgan Hill, CA

50 cloves fresh garlic (about 4 heads)
2 teaspoons salt
4 cups shredded Cheddar cheese (about 1 lb.)
5 quarts popped corn (about ½ cup unpopped corn)

Peel garlic and mince with salt to prevent sticking and to absorb garlic juices. Toss garlic with cheese. In large glass or plastic bowl, make alternate layers of popped corn and garlic-cheese mixture, coating popcorn as evenly as possible, especially at edge of bowl. Place in microwave oven and cook 1 minute. Shake bowl gently; turn 180 degrees and cook 1 more minute. Do not overcook. Immediately turn out onto cookie sheet, and quickly shape into plum-size balls. Set balls on sheets of waxed paper. Makes 4 dozen popcorn balls.

When was the last time you saw a vampire in Gilroy?

D.H.

HOMEMADE DOG BISCUITS

The following testimonials came from those who tested this recipe: "My 10-year-old Samoyed preferred them to those purchased at the store." "My daughter's 7-year-old, large dog liked them." "My son-in-law's 5-year-old beagle, a finicky eater, loved them." They are an excellent nutritious treat for the family dog and won't hurt the small children in the family if they happen to eat one.

Recipe contest entry: G. C. Bemis, Pebble Beach, CA

3½ cups all-purpose flour
2 cups whole wheat flour
2 cups bran
1 cup rye flour
1 cup grits or cornmeal
½ cup nonfat dry milk
1 tablespoon dehydrated minced or powdered garlic
4 teaspoons salt, optional (salt substitute may be used)
1 pkg. dry yeast
¼ cup warm water
2 cups tomato juice (salt free, if desired)

Combine all dry ingredients. Dissolve yeast in warm water and add tomato juice. Mix with dry ingredients. Dough should be very stiff. Knead dough for about 3 minutes. Roll out on floured board to ¼ to ½ inch thickness. Cut to desired size with knife or cookie cutters. Place on ungreased cookie sheet and bake at 300 degrees for 1 hour. Turn off oven. Leave biscuits overnight or at least 4 hours to harden. Makes about 7 dozen cookie-size biscuits.

Garlic very versatile, puts zing in bland dishes.

Shreveport, *Los Angeles Times*

BASIC GARLIC BUTTER

½ cup butter
2 to 3 cloves fresh garlic,
pressed or finely minced

Cream butter. Add garlic and beat until fluffy. Makes ½ cup.

Garlic Herb Butters:

Add freshly chopped chives, shallots or parsley to basic garlic butter, or select herbs and spices from the spice shelf—Italian herb seasoning, basil, or dill, for example.

Garlic Cheese Butters:

Add shredded or grated cheese of your choice to basic garlic butter.

Quickie Garlic Butter:

Use ¾ teaspoon garlic powder instead of fresh garlic. Add ¼ teaspoon salt and a dash black pepper. Let stand for 30 minutes for flavors to blend.

Easy Melt Garlic Butter:

Instead of creaming basic garlic butter, just heat butter and garlic over low heat until butter melts. Do not brown!

Extra Garlicky Butter:

Mash 6 cloves (or use dehydrated equivalent) of fresh garlic into ½ cup butter.

Delicate Garlic Butter:

Blanch and drain 4 cloves of fresh garlic and pound together; combine with ½ cup fresh butter or margarine. Pass the mixture through a fine sleeve.

Party Time Garlic Butter:

Moisten 1 teaspoon of instant granulated garlic with an equal amount of water. Place in a mixer bowl with 1 lb. softened butter or margarine. Beat until very creamy. Let stand about 20 minutes to blend flavors. Butter may also be melted over hot water or in a food warmer and spread with a pastry brush. Makes enough garlic butter for 100 medium pieces of French or Italian bread or 200 slices of bread or bun halves for sandwiches.

Gourmet Alley

The most popular attraction, however, was Gourmet Alley, a crescent of food booths backed up against a wall of wind-breaking poplars behind the hacienda. Here (one saw) a fast-working, sweat-dappled crew running about a foundry-like outdoor kitchen of homemade barbecue grills and primitive gas-fired stoves.

The fare they were turning out, however, had all the style, appearance, texture, flavor and appeal of continental cuisine patiently cooked in the stainless-steel kitchen of a gourmet restaurant.

MIKE DUNNE, Sacramento *Bee*

167

GOURMET ALLEY GARLIC BREAD

½ cup each butter and margarine
½ cup oil
3 cloves fresh garlic, minced
½ teaspoon pepper
¼ teaspoon oregano
½ cup white wine
3 tablespoons fresh parsley, chopped
2 loaves sweet French bread

Melt butter and margarine in pan. Add oil and garlic. Simmer over low heat for 1 minute. Add pepper, oregano and wine. Bring to a boil. Add parsley. Remove immediately from heat, and pour into large baking pan. Cut loaves in half lengthwise. Toast on grill or under broiler until golden brown. Dip toasted halves, cut side down, in butter mixture. Serve immediately.

CENTRAL COAST STIR-FRY VEGETABLES

¼ cup carrots
¼ cup celery
¼ cup yellow crooked neck squash
¼ cup zucchini
¼ cup broccoli
¼ cup cauliflower
2 tablespoons oil
3 large cloves fresh garlic, minced
½ teaspoon salt
¼ teaspoon pepper
Pinch red chili pepper
¼ teaspoon each basil and oregano
¼ cup dry white wine
1 tablespoon fresh parsley, chopped
¼ lemon

Cut carrots, celery, squash and zucchini into ½ x 2-inch pieces. Break broccoli and cauliflower into small pieces. Heat oil until almost smoking. Add vegetables; stir to coat with oil. Add garlic, salt, peppers, basil and oregano. Simmer 1 minute. Add wine and simmer 2 minutes or until vegetables are cooked *al dente*. Add parsley and squeeze in juice of lemon and serve immediately.

RUBINO'S STUFFED MUSHROOMS

Rancher/Chef Jim Rubino shares his recipe for the stuffed mush-rooms that were a hit at the Festival's Gourmet Alley. These mush-rooms make great finger appetizers for company but don't forget your family too). Prepare them the day before or at the last minute but be sure to make plenty for they'll quickly disappear.

Courtesy of: Jim Rubino, San Martin, CA

1 cup butter
⅓ cup crushed garlic
1 lb grated parmesan cheese
⅓ cup chopped parsley
50 large mushrooms

Melt butter, stir in crushed garlic, grated cheese and parsley. Mix well. Brush mushrooms clean, remove stem leaving center of mushroom empty. Stuff mush-room smoothing top. Place on broiler pan, stuffing side up, and broil until top turns golden brown. Serve out of the broiler!

PASTA CON PESTO ALLA PELLICCIONE

Paul Pelliccione, one of the head chefs of Gourmet Alley, shares his fabulous recipe for pasta con pesto as it was prepared for the Garlic Festival.

Courtesy of: Paul Pelliccione, Gilroy

2 cups packed fresh basil leaves, washed and well drained
1½ cups grated Romano cheese, plus additional cheese, if desired
½ cup olive oil
½ cup melted butter
6 large cloves fresh garlic, crushed
1 lb. spaghetti, flat noodles or similar pasta, cooked according to package directions

Place basil, 1 cup of the cheese, oil, butter and garlic in blender. Begin blending, turning motor on and off. Push pesto down from sides of blender with rubber spatula and continue until you have a very coarse puree. Makes about 1½ cups pesto. Spoon 1 cup pesto sauce over freshly cooked spaghetti. Mix quickly with two forks. Add ½ cup cheese and mix. Serve with addi-tional pesto sauce and cheese. Cover and refrigerate any leftover pesto up to a week, or freeze in small portions. The surface will darken when exposed to air, so stir the pesto before serving.

GARLIC FESTIVAL AND STEAK SANDWICHES

The aroma of gently sauteeing garlic brought on hunger pangs and set mouths watering. Those who attended the Garlic Festival are still talking about the Pepper Beefsteak Sandwiches served in Gourmet Alley. Chef Lou Trinchero and his team of cooks served 700 pounds of top sirloin, 250 pounds of green peppers and 750 loaves of French bread. Thank goodness Lou has worked the recipe down to one which will "feed 4 generously." You'll want to have plenty because they are unbelieveably delicious.

Courtesy of: Lou Trinchere, Gilroy

8 bell peppers, seeded and sliced in quarters
1 medium-sized onion, chopped
3 cloves fresh garlic, minced
   Salt and pepper to taste
   Olive oil
¾ lb. top sirloin steak, barbecued or broiled to desired degree of doneness
8 French rolls, halved and basted with garlic butter
   Garlic butter (see Miscellaneous section)

In skillet saute peppers, onion, garlic and salt and pepper in olive oil until tender. Brush rolls with garlic butter and heat in the oven or toast lightly under the broiler or over the barbecue. Slice steak thin and place on bottom half of roll. Top with pepper-garlic mixture and other half of roll. Makes 8 sandwiches.

Now garlic is to Gilroy what Mardi Gras is to New Orleans . . .

Los Angeles Herald-Examiner

CALAMARI, FESTIVAL-STYLE

One of Gourmet Alley's greatest attractions is watching the preparation of calamari. Some argue that eating it is even better. Here is Head Chef Val Filice's recipe for calamari as it is served at the Festival.

Courtesy of: Val Filice, Gilroy

3 lbs. calamari, (squid) cleaned and cut
⅓ cup olive oil
¼ cup white sherry
1 tablespoon crushed fresh garlic
½ lemon
1 teaspoon dry basil or 1 tablespoon fresh
1 teaspoon dry oregano or 1 tablespoon fresh
¼ teaspoon dry crushed red pepper
Red Sauce (below)

In large skillet heat olive oil at high heat. Add wine and sherry and saute crushed garlic. Squeeze the juice of ½ lemon into pan and place lemon rind in pan. Sprinkle herbs over and add calamari. Saute calamari for approximately 4 minutes on high heat. Do not overcook.

Red Sauce
1 lb. whole, peeled tomatoes, canned or fresh
1 tablespoon olive oil
½ green pepper, chopped
1 stalk celery, chopped
1 medium-sized yellow onion, chopped
3 cloves fresh garlic, minced

Mash tomatoes with potato masher and set aside. In medium-size pan heat oil, add chopped ingredients and saute until onion is transparent. Add mashed tomatoes and simmer for ½ hour. Pour red sauce over calamari and heat for 1 minute.

SCAMPI IN BUTTER SAUCE

A festival favorite, Scampi in Butter Sauce is another Gourmet Alley delicacy. The recipe here is courtesy of Val Filice who has served this exceptional dish to the delight of friends and family for years. Scampi, by the way, are a close relative of the shrimp but have no exact equivalent outside Italian waters. Substitute prawns or shrimp of medium to large size.

Courtesy of: Val Filice, Gilroy

Butter Sauce
- ½ to 1 cup butter
- 1 tablespoon finely minced fresh garlic
- 8 oz. clam juice
- ¼ cup flour
- 1 tablespoon minced parsley
- ⅓ cup white wine
  Juice of ½ lemon
- 1 teaspoon dry basil
- ¼ teaspoon nutmeg
  Salt and pepper to taste
- ½ cup half-and-half

Melt butter with garlic in small sauce pan over medium heat; do not let butter brown. In a separate bowl, mix clam juice, flour and parsley, blending until mixture is smooth. Pour flour mixture into garlic butter and stir until smooth and well blended. Stir in wine, lemon juice, herbs and spices, stirring constantly. Gradually add half-and-half and stir until thickened. Simmer for ½ hour to 45 minutes.

Scampi
- 2 tablespoons butter
- ⅓ cup olive oil
- 1 tablespoon minced fresh garlic
  Juice of 1 lemon (retain rind)
- 1 tablespoon fresh chopped parsley or 1 teaspoon dry
- ½ teaspoon crushed red pepper
- 1 tablespoon fresh basil or 1 teaspoon dry
- ¼ cup white wine
  Dash of dry vermouth
  Salt and pepper to taste
- 3 lbs. deveined and cleaned scampi (prawns)

Melt butter in large saucepan on high heat and add oil. Combine remaining ingredients keeping scampi aside until last minute. Add scampi and saute until firm and slightly pink. Do not over cook. Pour 1 cup of scampi butter over scampi. Refrigerate the rest for later use.

Tips and Tricks
To Do with Garlic

CHEF'S CHOICE
GARLIC

Garlic is more
than a fad. It's a
phenomenon.

Kim Upton
Chicago Sun Times

KNOW YOUR GARLIC!

Fresh garlic may be creamy white or have a purplish-red cast, but whatever the color, it should be plump and firm, with its paperlike covering intact, not spongy, soft or shriveled.

Dehydrated or other forms of processed garlic should be purchased in tightly sealed containers, preferably from markets where there is sufficient traffic to ensure that the spices are fresh.

HOW BEST TO STORE

Fresh garlic keeps best in a cool, dry place with plenty of ventilation. It should not be refrigerated unless you separate the cloves and immerse them in oil, either peeled or unpeeled. If the garlic isn't peeled, the cloves will hold their firmness longer, but peeling will be more difficult. Fresh garlic which is held in open-air storage for any length of time will lose some of its pungency and may even develop sprouts. The garlic is still usable, but will be somewhat milder and more will be needed to achieve the same strength of flavor in a dish being prepared.

Dehydrated forms of garlic should be stored with other spices in as cool and dry a place as possible, definitely not above or next to the kitchen range, sink or in front of a window with exposure to the sun. Keep tightly sealed. Processed garlic which requires refrigeration after opening should, of course, always be stored in the refrigerator to maintain its quality.

HOW TO PEEL

If you are peeling only a few cloves, simply press each clove against the cutting board with the flat side of a heavy kitchen knife or press between the thumb and forefinger to loosen the skin first. If your recipe calls for a larger quantity of garlic, drop the cloves in boiling water for just a minute and drain quickly. They will peel quite easily. If you have a microwave oven, you can cook the cloves for 5 seconds or so to achieve the same effect.

MUST GARLIC BE PEELED?

Not necessarily. You can cook unpeeled garlic in a hot pan—it won't burn easily—then slip off the skins when the garlic is soft. Or, if the garlic is to be cooked in a soup or sauce and then the whole cloves discarded, there is certainly no necessity to peel them. And, if you are preparing a dish such as "Forty Clove Chicken," cook the cloves unpeeled and then simply press the soft garlic out of the skin with your fingers or with knife and fork as you eat it.

WHICH TO USE

Whether you use fresh, dehydrated, or processed garlic is a matter of personal choice. Fresh garlic fans note that garlic flavors food differently, depending on how it is used. Fresh uncooked garlic is most pungent when pureed, crushed or finely minced. For milder garlic flavor, keep cloves whole or cut in large pieces. Whole cloves cooked for a long time with roasts, stews or soups have a surprisingly sweet, nutlike flavor. It is very important when cooking with fresh garlic not to burn it. When garlic is burned, it has a very bitter flavor and must be discarded or it will ruin the flavor of the dish. Remember, when sauteeing garlic in oil, keep the heat fairly low and cook it until it is just very lightly browned.

Other forms of garlic vary somewhat in their flavoring characteristics, but you can generally plan on the following substitutions:

1 average-size clove of fresh garlic	= ⅛ teaspoon dehydrated, powdered, minced or chopped garlic
	or
	½ teaspoon garlic salt. (*Caution:* when using garlic salt in recipes calling for fresh garlic, decrease the amount of salt called for.)

GARLIC ODOR

Several techniques help to control the odor of garlic on the hands that results from peeling or chopping. Disposable plastic gloves can be worn while performing this chore. Or you can rub the fingers with salt and lemon juice afterwards, then rinse under cold water. The best solution we have found is to rub the fingers over the bowl of a stainless steel teaspoon under running water for a few moments. There is a chemical reaction which takes place that does indeed eliminate the odor from the fingers. The more garlic chopped the longer it will take to remove the odor, but it can be done! Garlic odor on the breath is most easily controlled by eating fresh parsley. Parsley has been called "nature's mouthwash" by garlic lovers because of its effectiveness. Chewing on a coffee bean or two also seems to do the trick.

TO CHOP OR PRESS?

There are some who swear by their garlic press and others who claim that using a garlic press makes the fresh garlic taste bitter. It is certainly a quick and easy method of mincing garlic; however, you do lose some of the pulp which means that hand-chopped gives a better yield and less waste. Again, the choice is yours. If you choose to chop the garlic by hand, here's a tip from the wife of a garlic grower: Add the salt required for your recipe directly into the minced garlic while it is still on the cutting board. The salt will absorb the juices and make it easier to scoop the tiny garlic pieces off the board.

GARLIC FLAVORED OIL, VINEGAR OR SALT

It's easy to flavor with garlic by adding peeled whole cloves of garlic to bottles of oil or vinegar for two or three days before using. To make garlic salt, just bury 3 peeled and pressed garlic cloves in half a cup of salt. Add fresh ground pepper and ground ginger to taste, if you like. Let stand for a few days in a screw-top jar. Remove garlic and use the salt as desired to flavor soups, meats, salads, etc.

GARLIC BUTTER

Make logs of garlic butter and freeze them to have on hand to melt on broiled meats or to mix into fresh cooked vegetables or spread on bread. Just add mashed garlic cloves or the equivalent in dehydrated or processed garlic to suit your taste to sticks of butter (about 6 cloves fresh garlic per stick is recommended). If you wish, add a few herbs and salt lightly. Form into logs, wrap in plastic and freeze. Slice off as needed.

BAKED WHOLE HEADS

One of the most popular ways to serve fresh garlic is to bake whole heads to serve as an hors d'oeuvre with crunchy bread or as an accompaniment to meat or vegetables. Peel as much of the outer skin away as possible, leaving the cloves unpeeled and the head intact. Place heads in covered casserole or on a piece of heavy aluminum foil, drizzle with olive oil, dot with butter, salt and pepper to taste and bake covered at 350 degrees for about 45 minutes or until cloves are soft and can be squeezed easily out of their skins onto bread or other foods.

SPECIAL TERMS

Bulb. The name for the usable portion of fresh garlic made up of as many as 15 or more individual cloves.

Clove. One of the several segments of a bulb, each of which is covered with a thin, papery skin.

Crushed. A term which refers to fresh garlic which has been smashed by the broad side of a knife or cleaver on a chopping board or with a rolling pin between several thicknesses of waxed paper.

Dehydrated. Any of several forms of garlic from which the moisture has been removed. Dehydrated garlic is available minced, powdered, and granulated.

Fresh. The term used to describe garlic which has not been dehydrated. Actually "fresh" garlic is allowed to "cure" in the field before harvesting just until the papery skin, not the cloves, becomes dry.

Garlic Braid. A garland of fresh garlic braided together by its tops. Braiding is done while the garlic is still only partially cured with some moisture remaining in the tops and before the tops are removed in harvesting. When they become fully dried, they are too brittle to braid. Originally devised as a convenient storage method quite decorative and have become popular in this country as a kitchen adornment. Serious garlic lovers like to use them for cooking purposes, cutting off one bulb at a time from the braid. Care should be taken if the braid is to be preserved as a decoration that it is not handled carelessly. The papery covering of the bulb is fragile and will break easily when the garlic itself has shriveled after a year or so.

Granulated. A dehydrated form of garlic that is five times stronger than raw garlic. Its flavor is released only in the presence of moisture.

Juice. Garlic juice may be purchased commercially or prepared by squeezing fresh cloves in a garlic press, being certain not to include any of the flesh. Juice blends easily for uniform flavor.

Minced. This term is used for both dehydrated and fresh garlic. Generally called for when small pieces of garlic are desirable as in soups, sauces or salad dressings. Fresh garlic may be minced using a sharp knife on a chopping board. If the recipe calls for salt, add it to the garlic while mincing. It will prevent the garlic from sticking to the knife and absorb the juices otherwise lost in the mincing process. Finely minced garlic, as called for in most French recipes, tends to disappear into the finished dish. For a more robust flavor, mince more coarsely as called for in many Chinese dishes. Large amounts of garlic can be minced using a blender or food processor.

Garlic is enveloping the country.

Twin Falls Idaho Times News

Powdered. Powdered garlic is available commercially. When using powder in recipes with a high acid content, mix with water (two parts water to one part powder) before adding. Powdered garlic can be made from fresh by slowly drying peeled garlic cloves in the oven. When very dry, pound or crush until fine and powdery. Pass through a sieve and pound any large pieces, then sieve again. Store in sealed jars in a dry place.

Pressed. A term for garlic which has been put through a garlic press. There are many different types of presses available, some even "self-cleaning." When using a garlic press, it isn't necessary to peel the garlic clove. Simply cut it in half and place in the press. Then squeeze. The skin will stay behind, making the press easier to clean. Remember to clean your press immediately after use before the small particles which remain behind have a chance to dry.

Puree. A term for garlic which has been cooked at high heat and then pressed through a sieve. Available commercially or made at home. It is excellent to have on hand to blend into soups, sauces or to spread on slices of bread to serve with hors d'oeuvres.

Garlic Salt. Available commercially, it is usually a blend of approximately 90% salt, approximately 9% garlic and approximately 1% free-flowing agent. When using garlic salt in recipes calling for fresh garlic, decrease the amount of salt called for.

No one is indifferent to garlic. People either love it or hate it, and most good cooks seem to belong to the first group.

Faye Levy
Los Angeles Herald Examiner

COOKING EQUIVALENTS TABLE

Kitchen Measure

$\quad$ 3 teaspoons = 1 tablespoon
$\quad$ 2 tablespoons = 1 fluid ounce
$\quad$ 16 tablespoons = 1 cup
$\quad$ 8 ounces = 1 cup or ½ pound
$\quad$ 16 ounces = 1 pound
$\quad$ 2 cups = 1 pint
$\quad$ 2 pints = 1 quart
$\quad$ 4 pints = 2 quarts or ½ gallon
$\quad$ 8 pints = 4 quarts or 1 gallon
$\quad$ 4 quarts = 1 gallon

Metric Measure

$\quad$ 1 ounce = 28.35 grams
$\quad$ 1 gram = .035 ounce
$\quad$ 8 ounces = 226.78 grams or ½ pound
$\quad$ 100 grams = 3½ ounces
$\quad$ 500 grams = 1 pound (generous)
$\quad$ 1 pound = ½ kilogram (scant)
$\quad$ 1 kilogram = 2¼ pounds (scant)
$\quad$ ⅒ liter = ½ cup (scant) or ¼ pint (scant)
$\quad$ ½ liter = 2 cups (generous) or 1 pint (generous)
$\quad$ 1 quart = 1 liter (scant, or .9463 liter)
$\quad$ 1 liter = 1 quart (generous, or 1.0567 quarts)
$\quad$ 1 liter = 4½ cups or 1 quart 2 ounces
$\quad$ 1 gallon = 3.785 liters (approximately 3¾ liters)

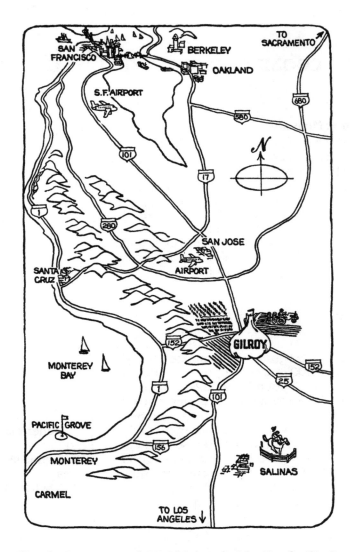

Gilroy, California is a town of 23,000 located in the fertile Santa Clara Valley, 80 miles south of San Francisco. Its livelihood is derived from a variety of agricultural products among which garlic is an especially important crop. It is estimated that garlic is a $53 million industry in Gilroy and within a 90-mile radius, 90 percent of the garlic grown and processed in the United States can be found. Gilroy is also the home of two of the major dehydration plants and three of the major fresh garlic shippers in the world. An estimated 100 million pounds of garlic is grown, processed or distributed through Gilroy each year. With all this in its favor and the desire to stage an unparalleled celebration of garlic that would attract garlic lovers from all over the world, Gilroy claimed the title Garlic Capital of the World during the first annual Festival in 1979.

Index

In many languages garlic means "good eating."

S.M. Fitzgerald
Gannett News Service

More great cookbooks

☐ *The Asparagus Cookbook* by the Stockton Asparagus Festival
Over 150 prize-winning asparagus recipes from a festival held in California's agricultural heartland, recipes for appetizers, soups, salads, main courses, and sauces. Other chapters cover artichoke history and lore, and a guide to the festival.
$9.95 paper, 160 pages

☐ *The Artichoke Cookbook* by Patricia Rain
"I love artichokes, and prepare them in at least three dozen different ways."
—M.F.K. Fisher
Many people, even those who love artichokes, never do anything more ambitious than steaming or boiling them. This book will expand your culinary horizons with over a hundred elegant recipes.
$11.95 paper, 180 pages

☐ *The Vanilla Cookbook* by Patricia Rain
Vanilla is an essential, if subtle, flavor in many foods, from simple desserts like ice cream and cookies to savory gourmet dishes like Scallops Paimpol, Chicken Curry, and Hollandaise Sauce. Includes a full-color photo insert showing the cultivation and manufacture of vanilla.
$11.95 paper

☐ *The Great Chile Book* by Mark Miller with John Harrisson
A full-color photographic guide to one hundred varieties of chile–fifty each of fresh and dried, including a brief description, tips for use, and a heat rating. The book also gives a history of the chile in Mexican and Southwestern tradition, and recipes from the Coyote Cafe.
$14.95 paper, 152 pages A TEN SPEED BOOK

☐ *The Great Chile Posters*
Created by Mark Miller o the Coyote Cafe, these sumptuous chile identification posters show thirty-one fresh chilies and thirty-five dried ones, with heat ratings and cooking tips for each. A fabulous addition to any wall, kitchen or otherwise.
Fresco (fresh chilies) $15. *Seco* (dried chilies) $15. **Both posters $25.**

Available from your local bookstore, or order direct from the publisher. Please include $3.50 shipping & handling for the first book, and 50 cents for each additional book. California residents include local sales tax. Write for our free complete catalog of over 400 books and tapes.

Ship to:

Name _____

Address _____

City_____ State _____Zip _____

Phone_____

Celestial Arts

P.O. Box 7123

Berkeley, CA 94707

For VISA, Mastercard or

American Express orders

call (800) 841-BOOK